DRAGON

FANCY

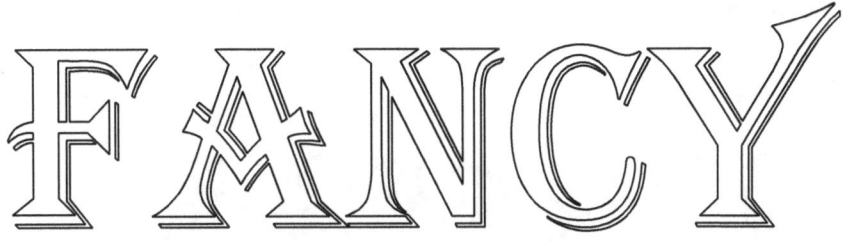

Please send queries to:

Julie Thompson
FeatherladyStudio1@gmail.com

ISBN: 0999422707
ISBN-13: 978-0999422700

DEDICATION

To all of you friends who watched this project begin from a single drawing and idea; whose un-waning enthusiasm helped me to carry it over the finish line – thank you. Your suggestions and support have led to this final copy you now hold in your hands.

A special thank you goes to dear friends whose enthusiasm and support for this project extended to Patreon. Their generous support was vital in helping to fund all the little expenses involved in creating and publishing this coloring book.

Nancy Johnson,
Graham Cross,
Audrey Oakes,
Geili Friedi.

An additional special thanks goes out to the colorists who allowed their work to be used on the back of the cover.

Nancy Johnson – contributed her version of "Moonlight Magic"
Peggi Rowe – contributed her version of "Dragon's Eye"

Thank you! This coloring book could not have made it to print without all of you.

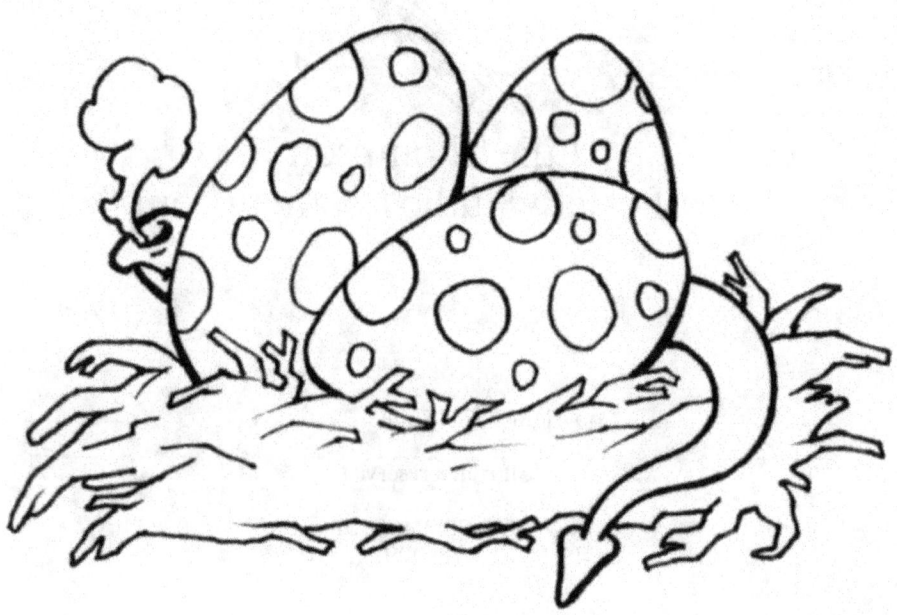

THIS BOOK BELONGS TO THE COLORING HORDE OF

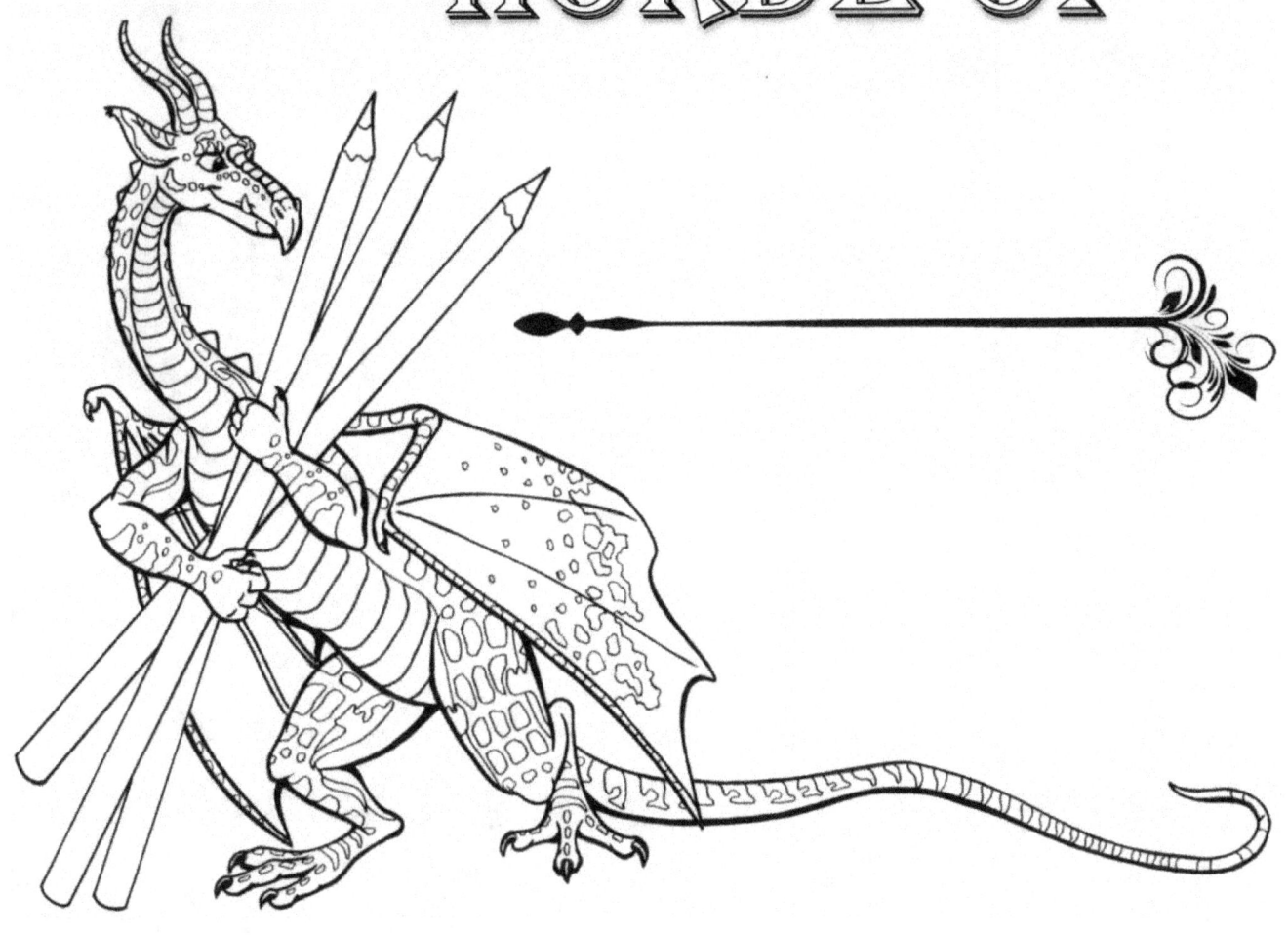

Table of Illustrations

"What… is your name?"
"What… is your quest?"
"What…is the airspeed velocity of an unladen swallow?"

In the Pacific Northwest, the native Kwakwa'awakw people tell the legends of a fearsome sea serpent. In their stories, Sisiutl has a head at each end, curled horns, and a more human-like face in the middle. This creature is highly poisonous, and the simple act of touching it will kill you. In searching for more information, I stumbled upon a creature in more contemporary stories with claims of sightings up and down our coast. The creature has been dubbed Cadborosaurus, or Caddy, for short. The beast has large eyes, a horse-like head, curved horns, and is described as having spikes or a mane down the length of its neck and back. I've combined both of these legends in this illustration.

Chinese dragons playing Mahjong.

Which one is the student? It's up to you! The cathedral ruins of Saint Andrews Scotland can be seen through the window.

This illustration gets its inspiration from the recent and bountiful discoveries of dinosaur fossils on the Isle of Skye in Scotland. You will see the towering rock formation known as the Old Man of Storr, which is on the Trotternish Peninsula on the north end of the island.

What would be a more suitable treasure hunting companion than a well-trained Griffin? The legends of Griffins came from the Steppe; the ancient nomadic people told of a fearsome lion/eagle creature that savagely protected their treasures. These tales were told to discourage would-be thieves, but the stories may have been inspired by the many Protoceratops fossils that can still be found in the region. This was a lion-sized dinosaur with a sharp beak at the end of its snout.

The islands of Hawai'i have their own set of dragon stories – fantastic creatures who are somewhere between a gecko and a Komodo dragon in appearance. Some shape-shift, some change size, but most seem to be protectors. Many thanks to Hawaiian musician Matt Sproat for sharing his family story from the island of Moloka'i, which I have illustrated in this book. For further information on that story, see the corresponding sketchbook entry on the page following this coloring illustration.

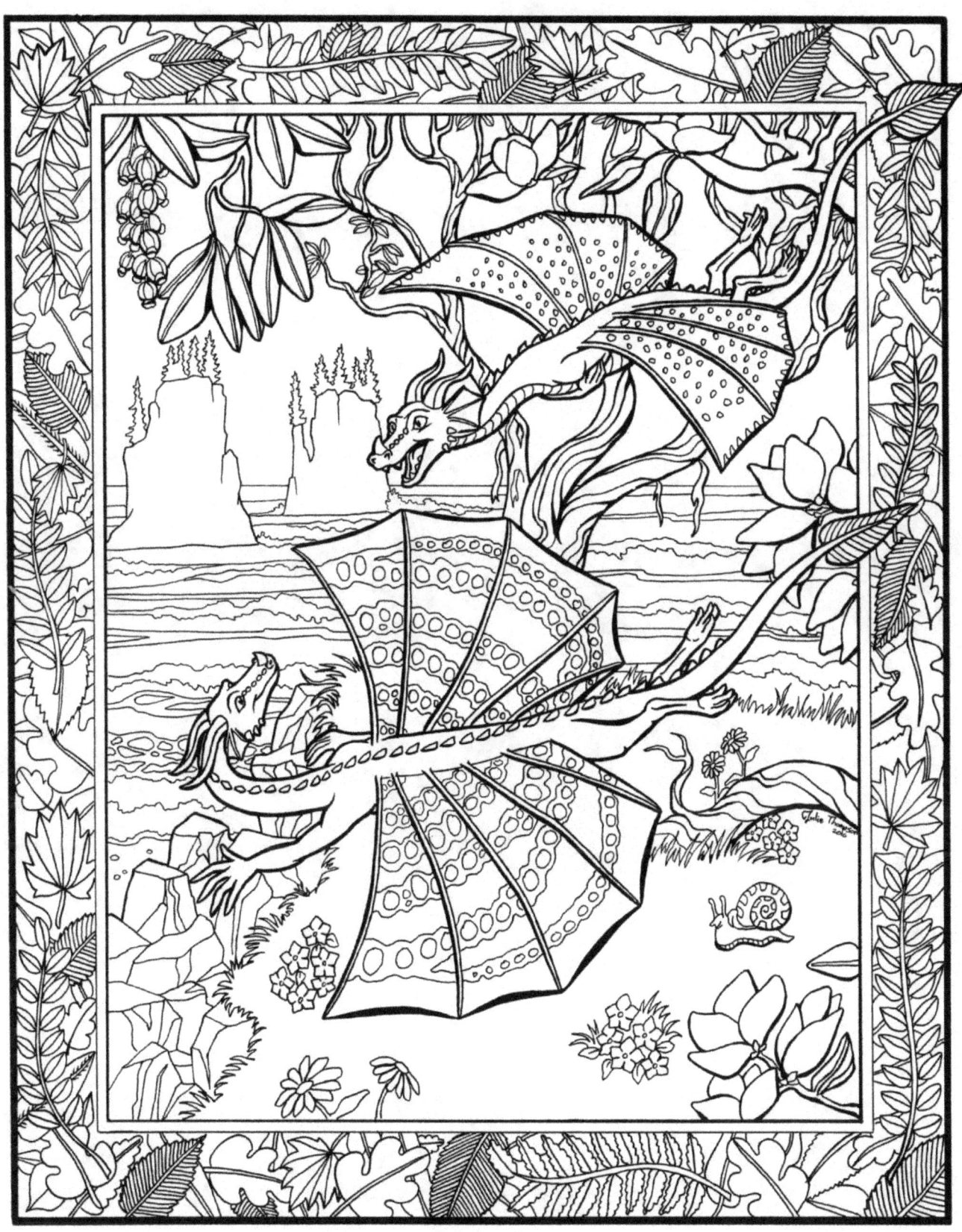

Seaside Glide

1

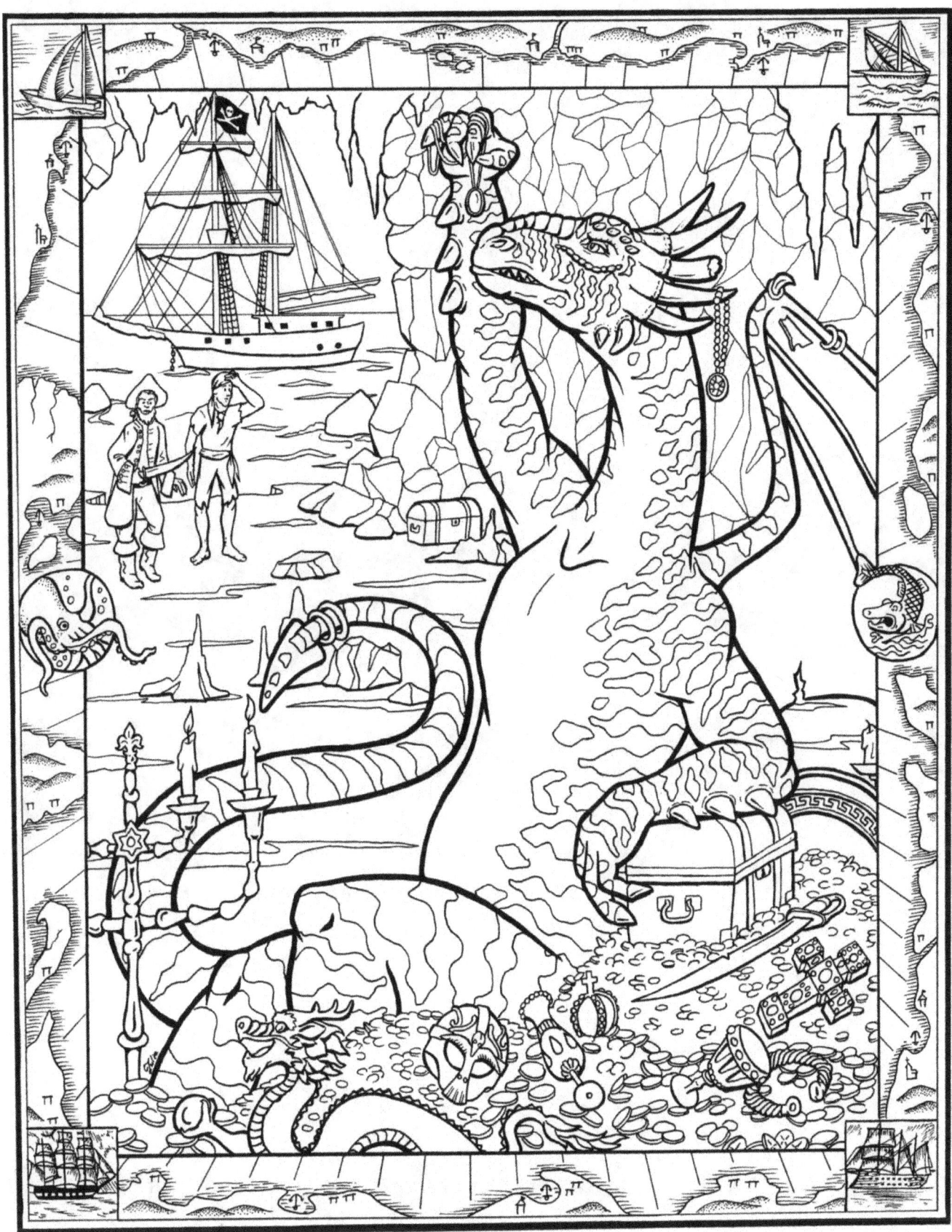

Pirates Plundered
2

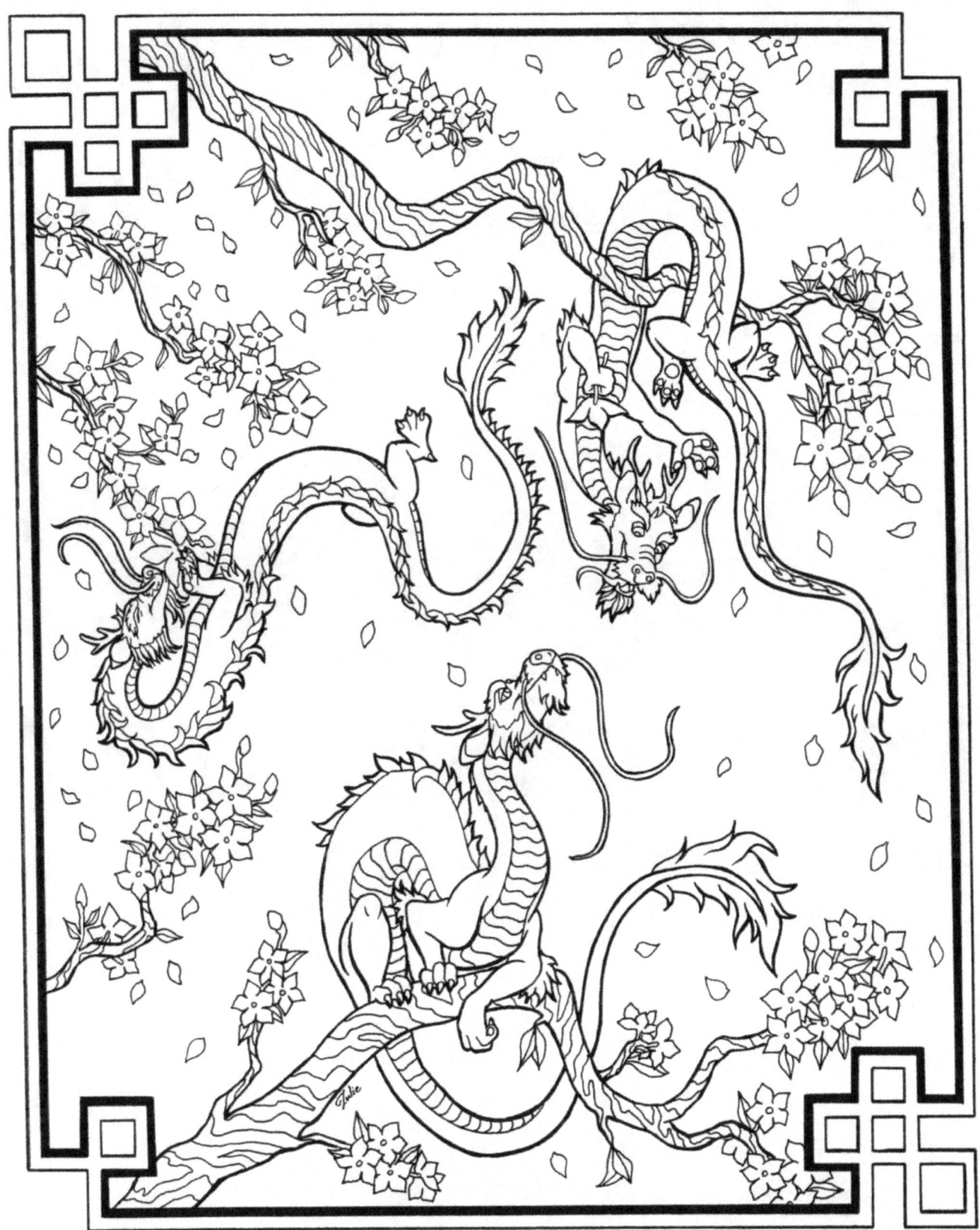

Stop and Smell the Flowers

3

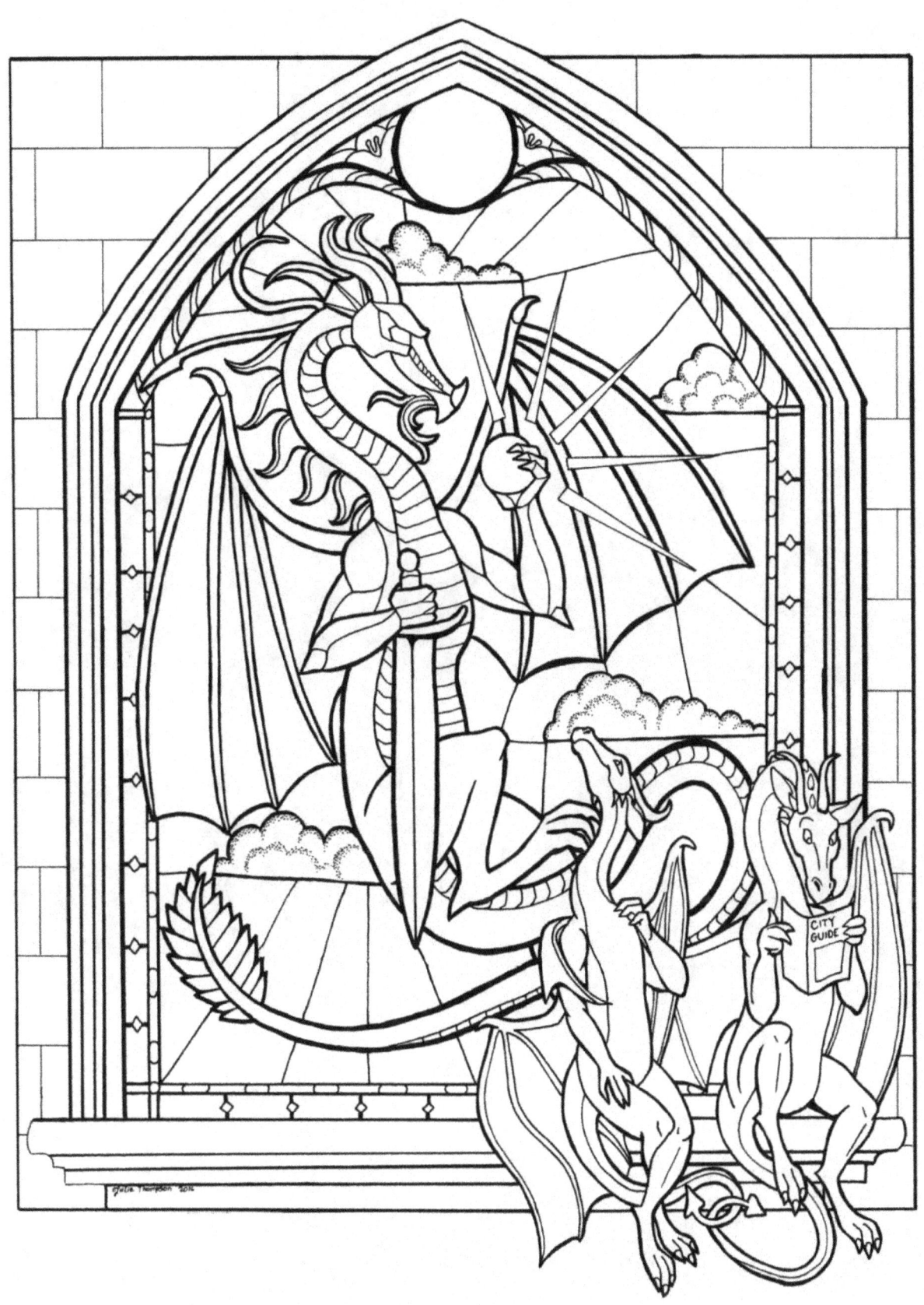

Sightseers
4

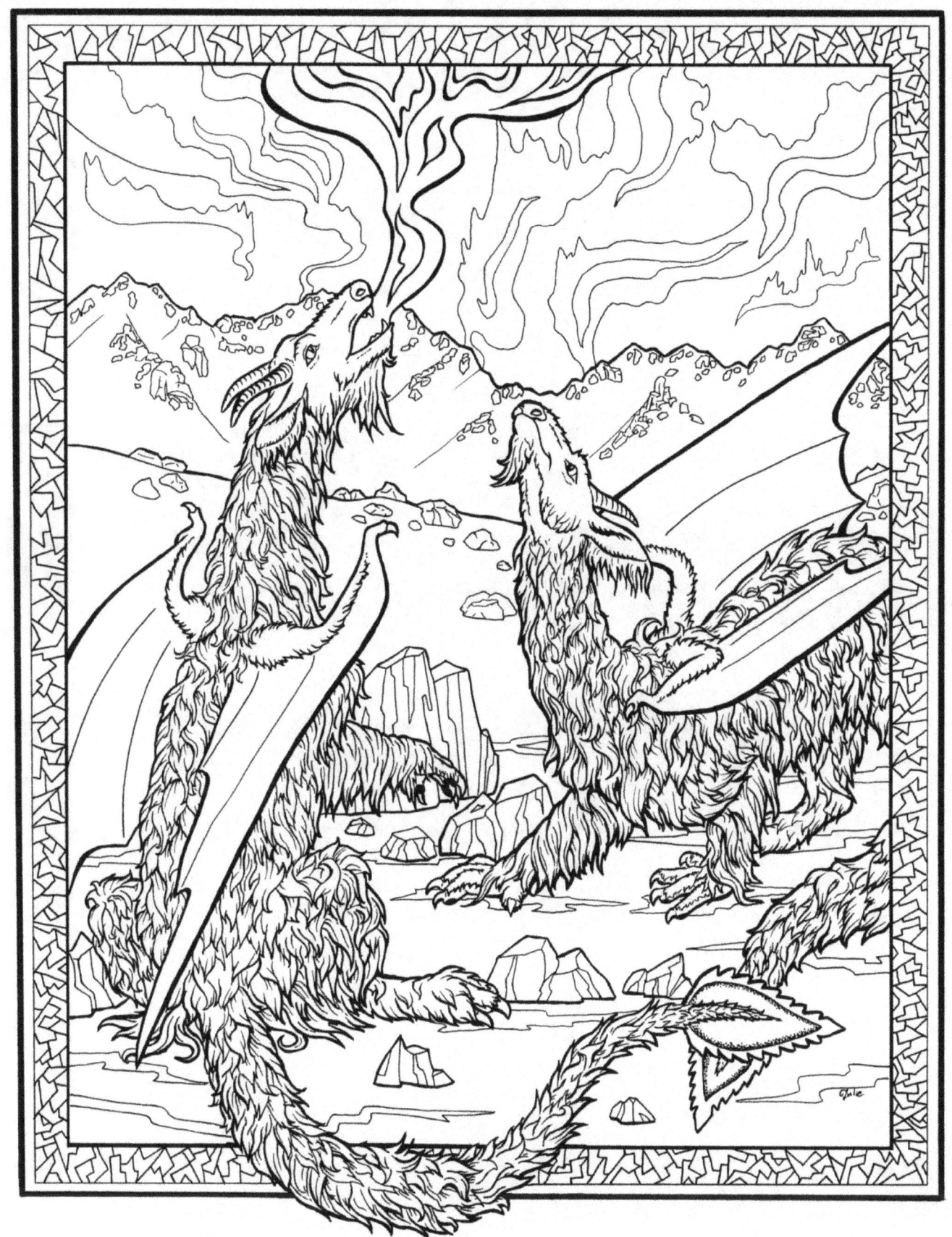

Coldfire
5

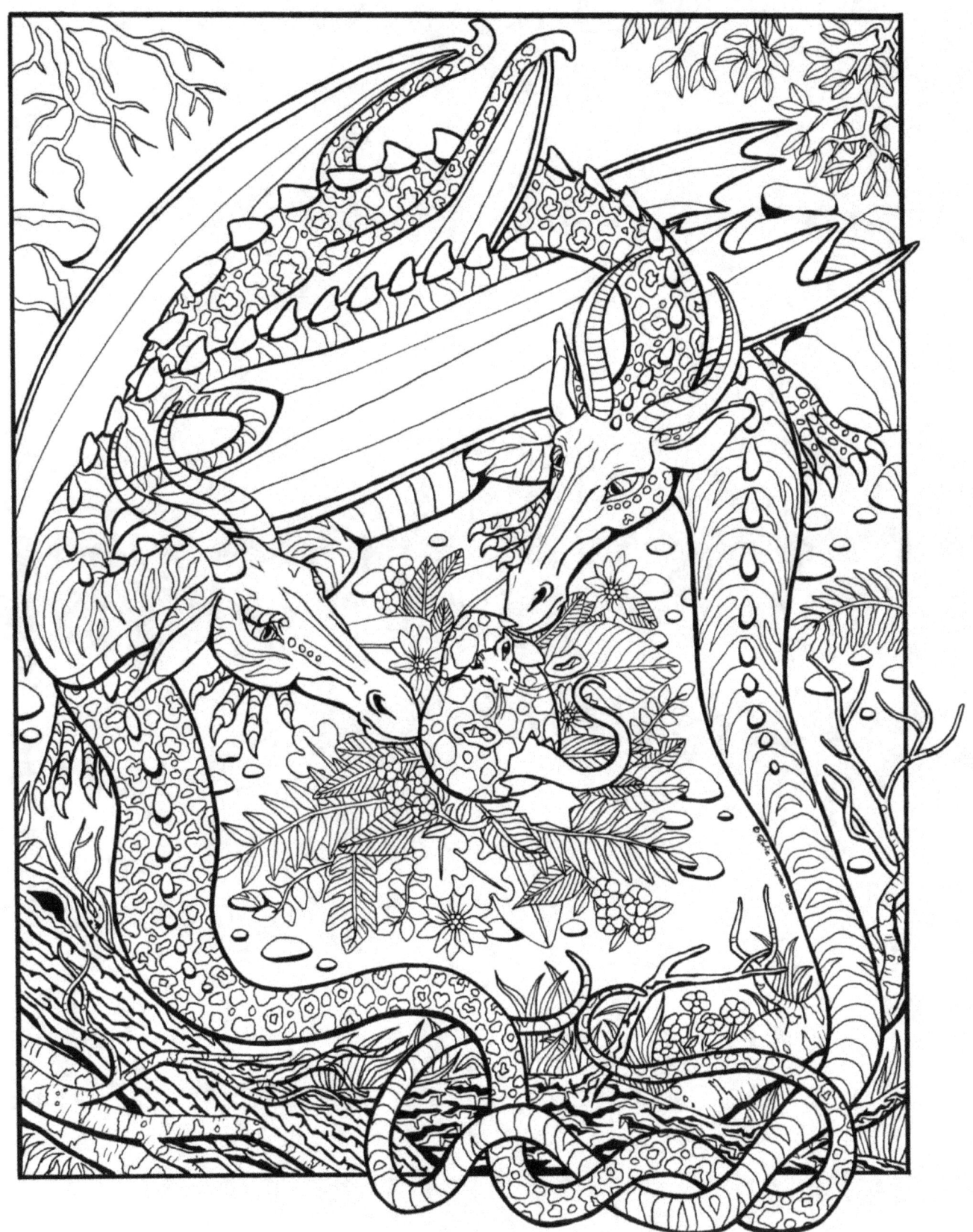

Baby's First Breath

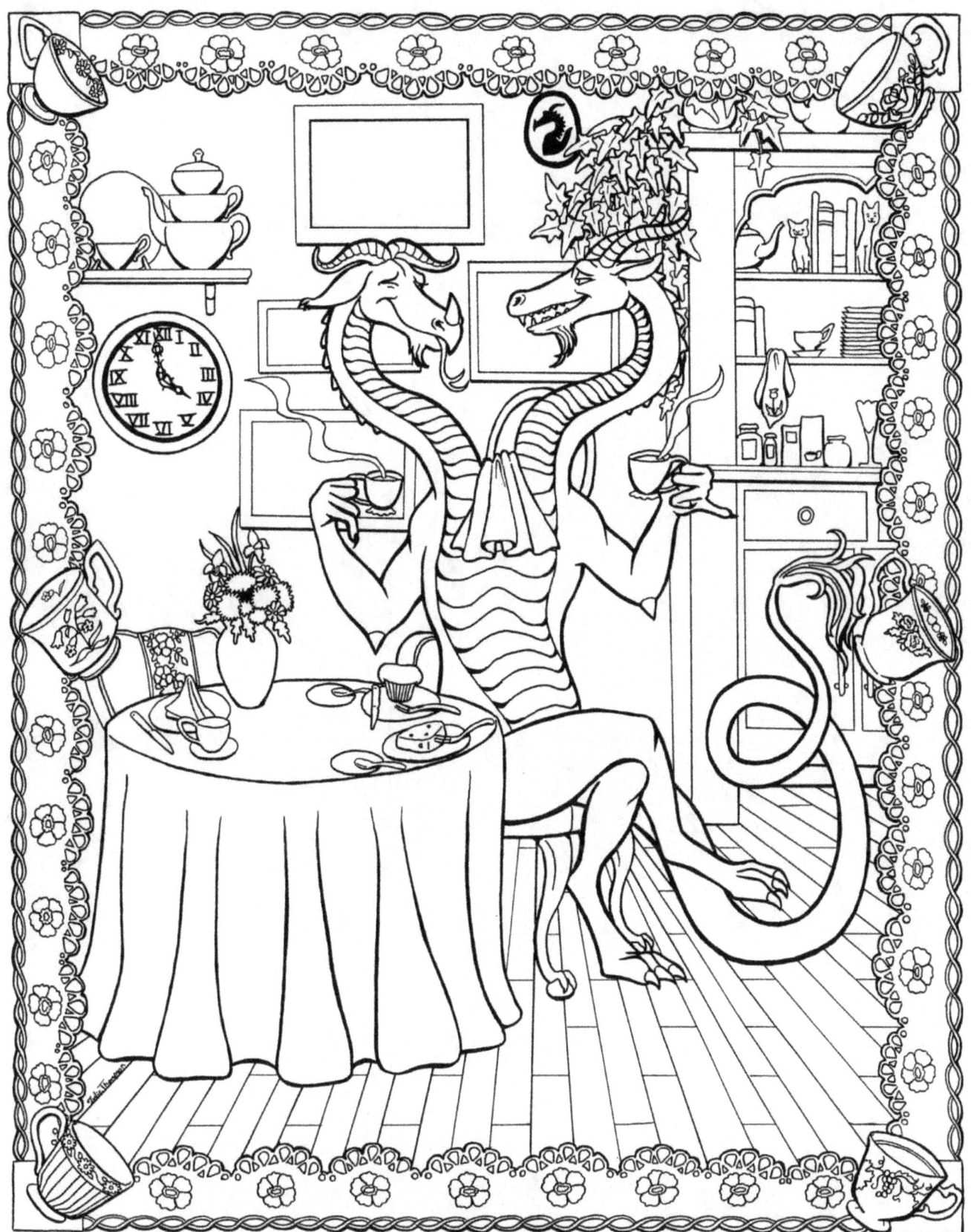

Tea for Two

7

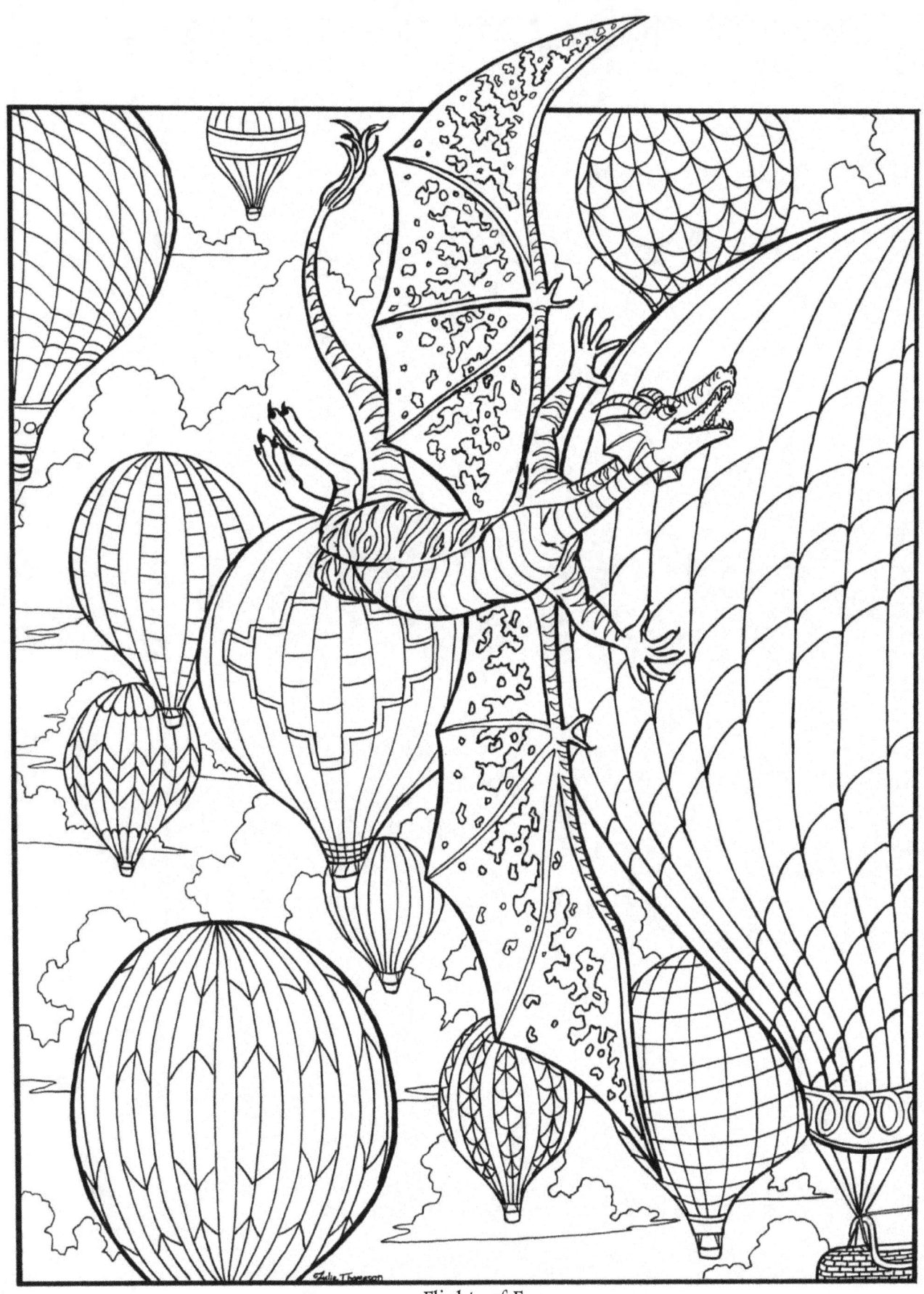

Flights of Fancy

8

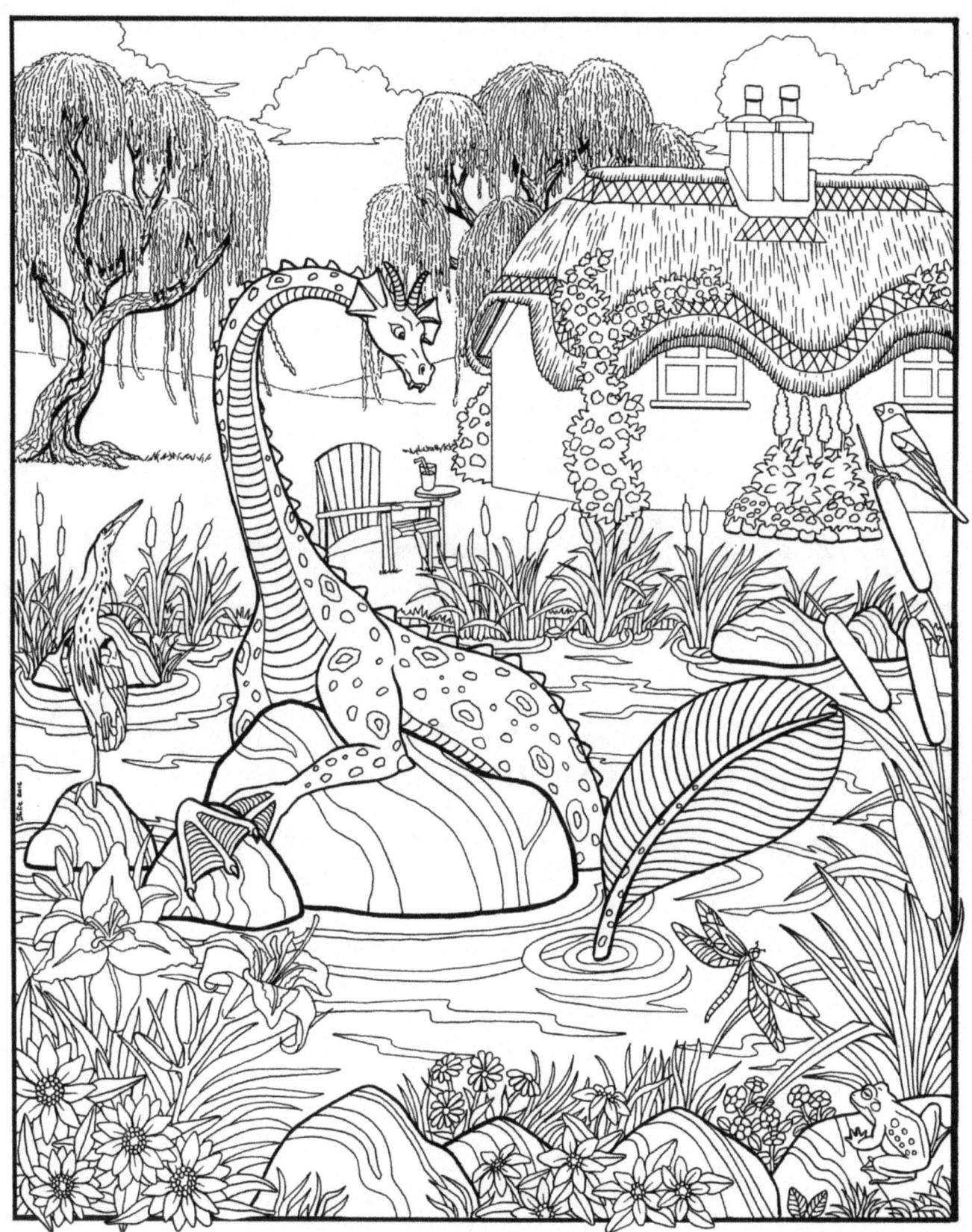

Sentinel

9

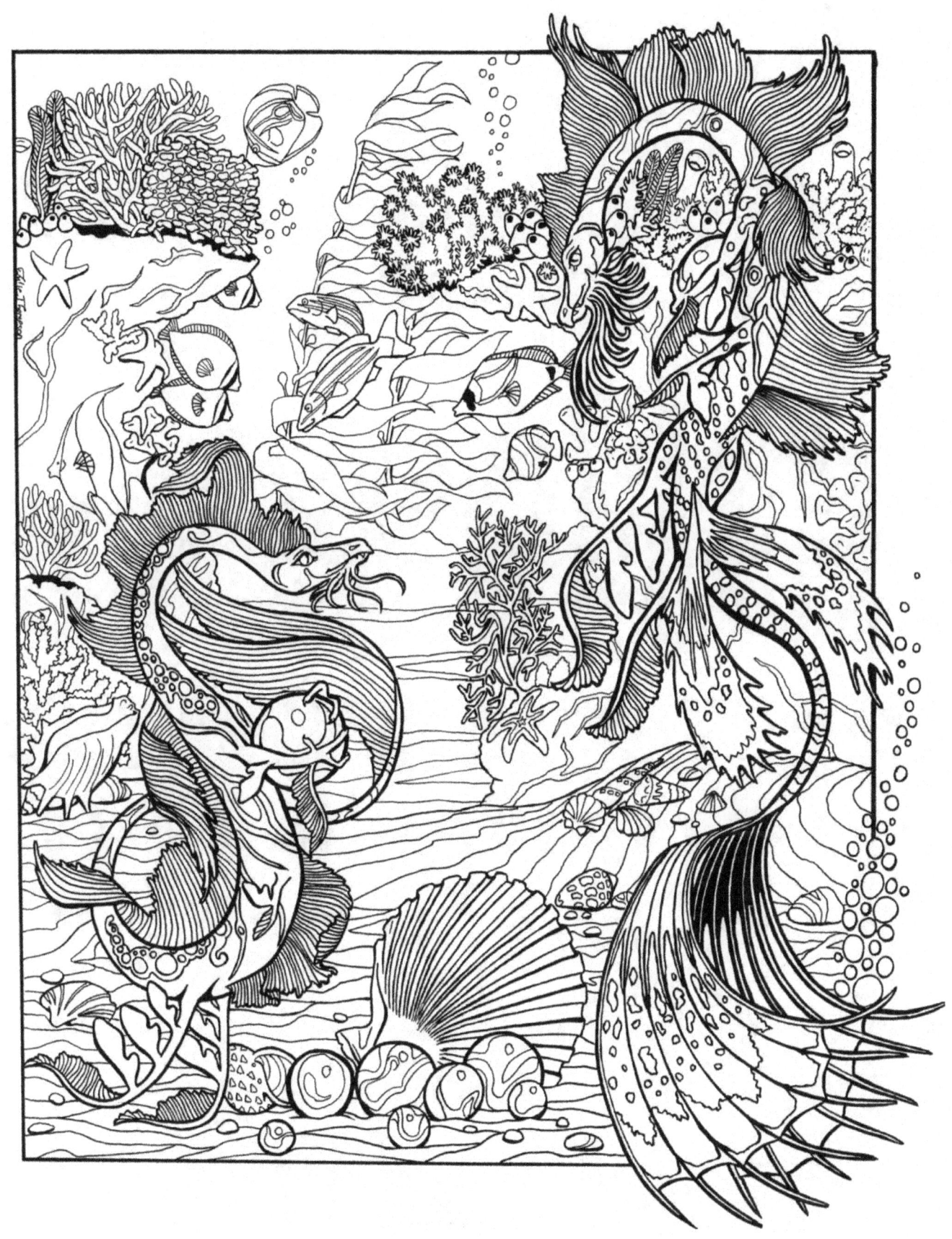

The Pearl Gatherers
10

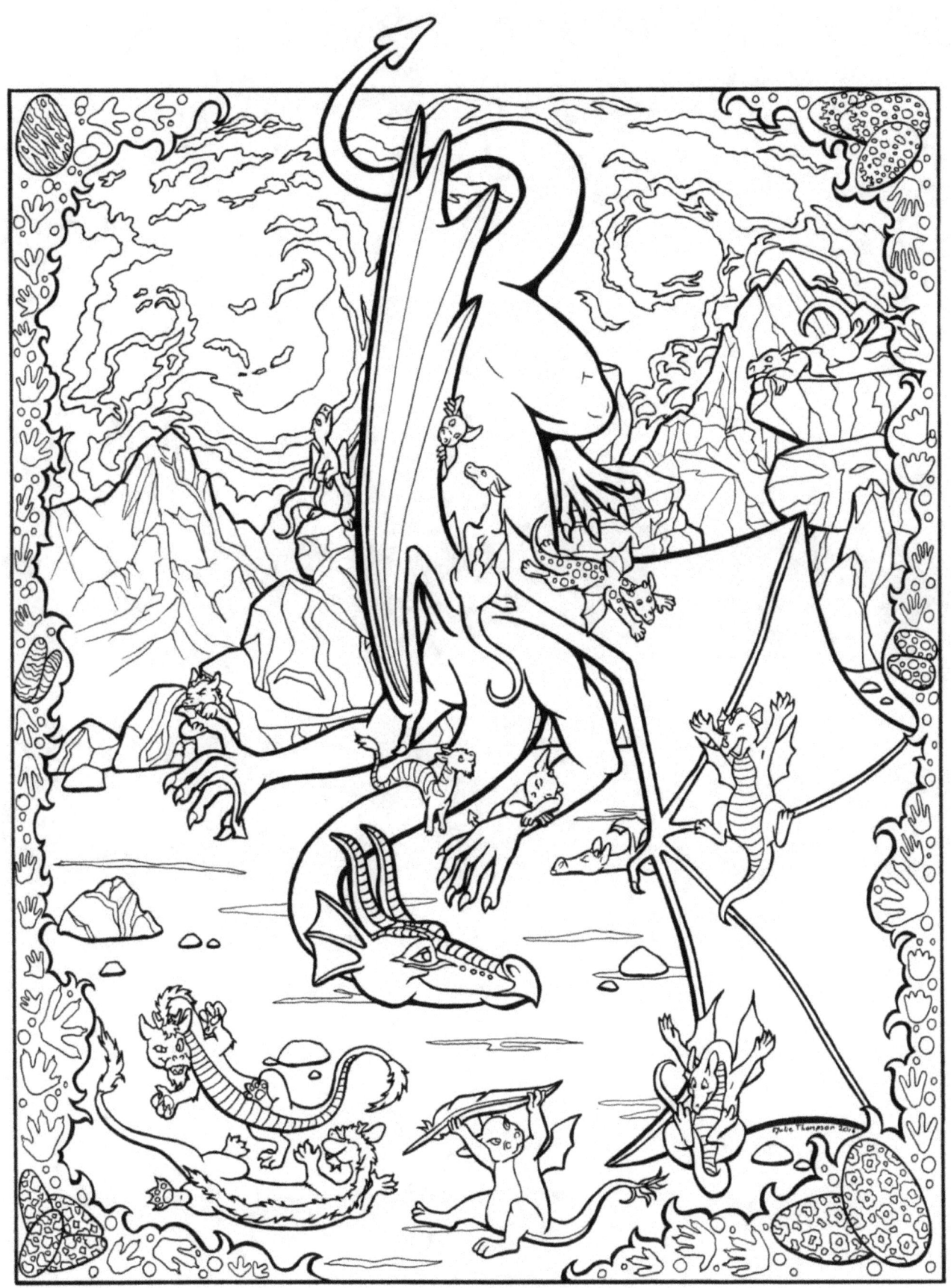

The Babysitter

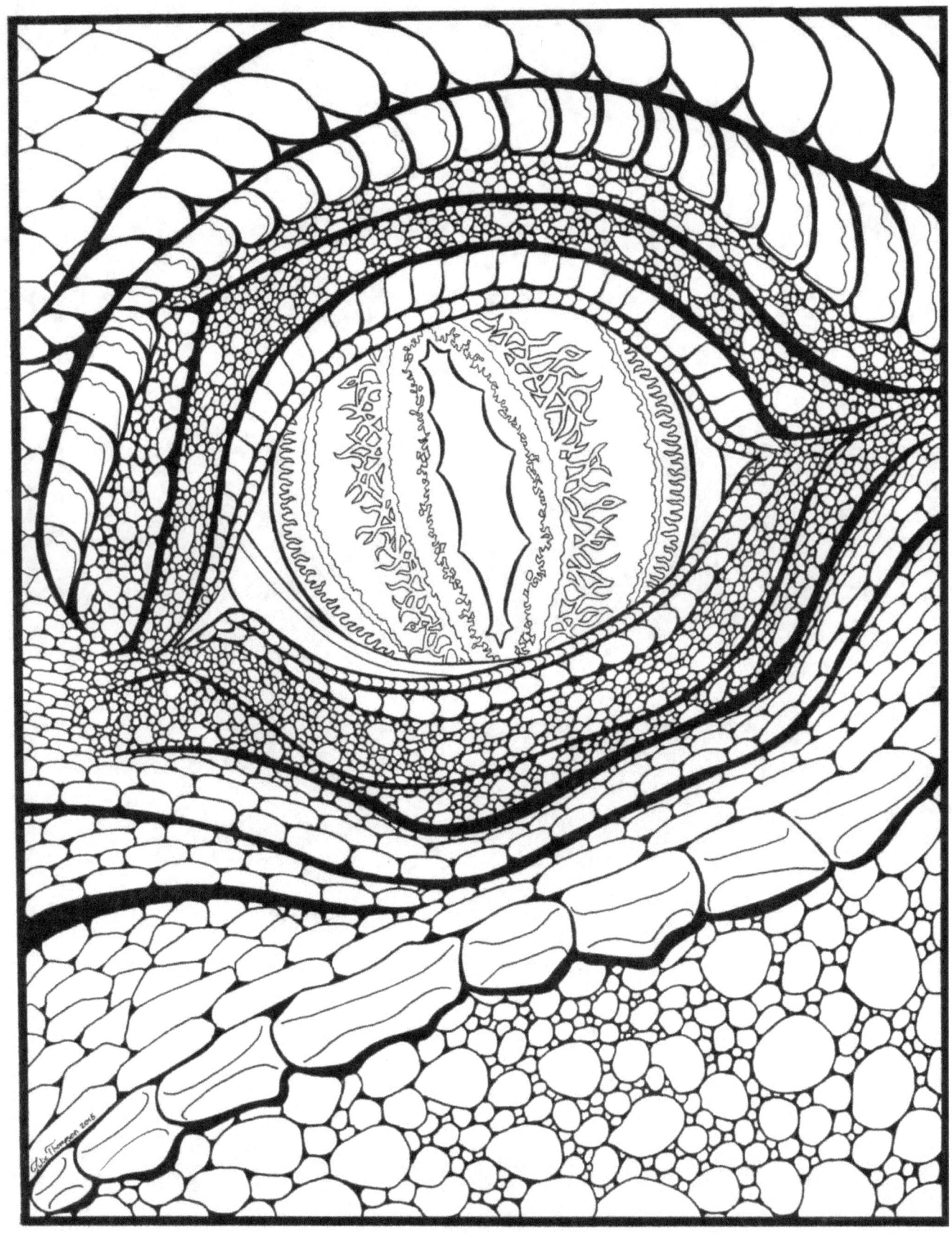

Dragon's Eye
12

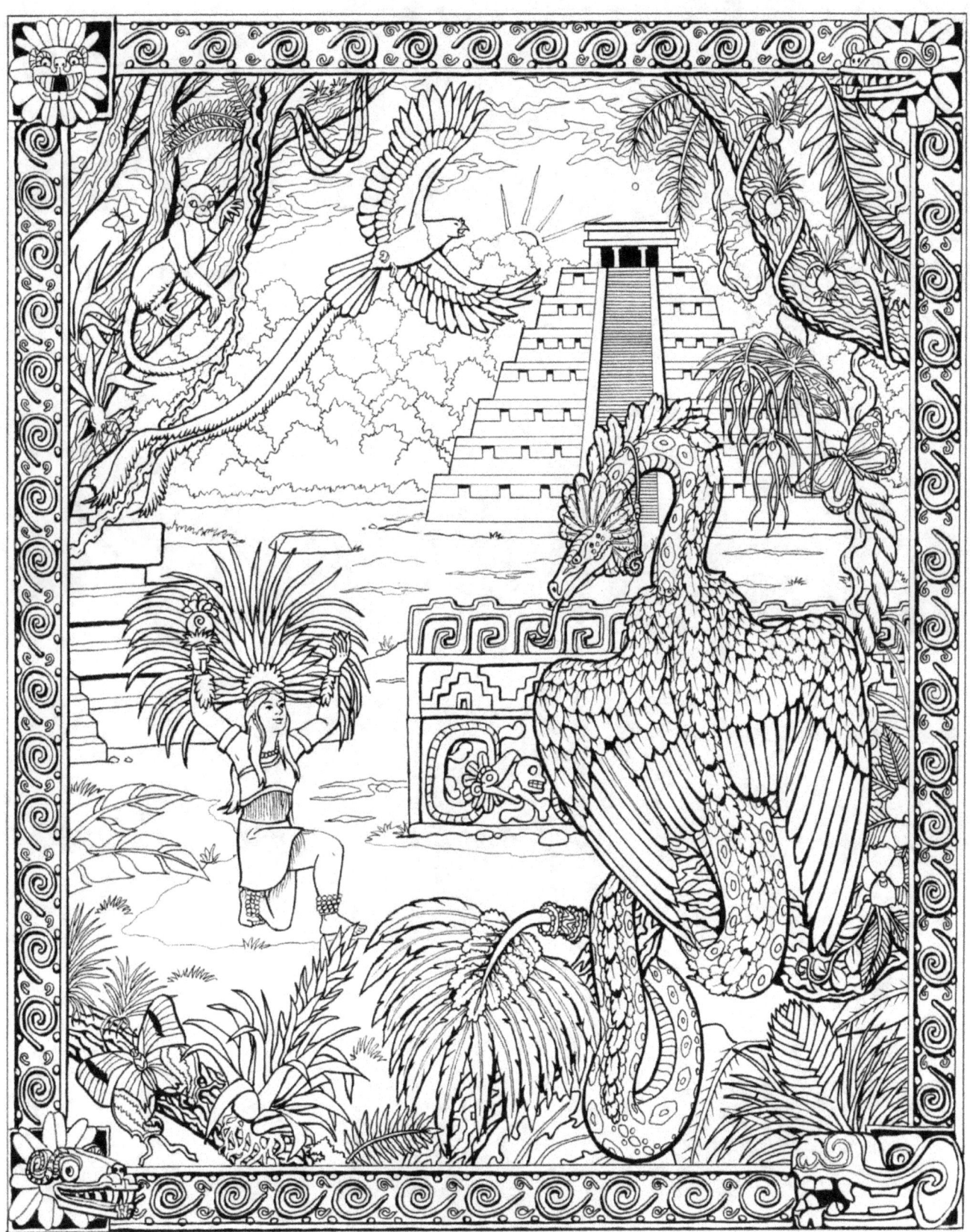

Quetzalcoatl

13

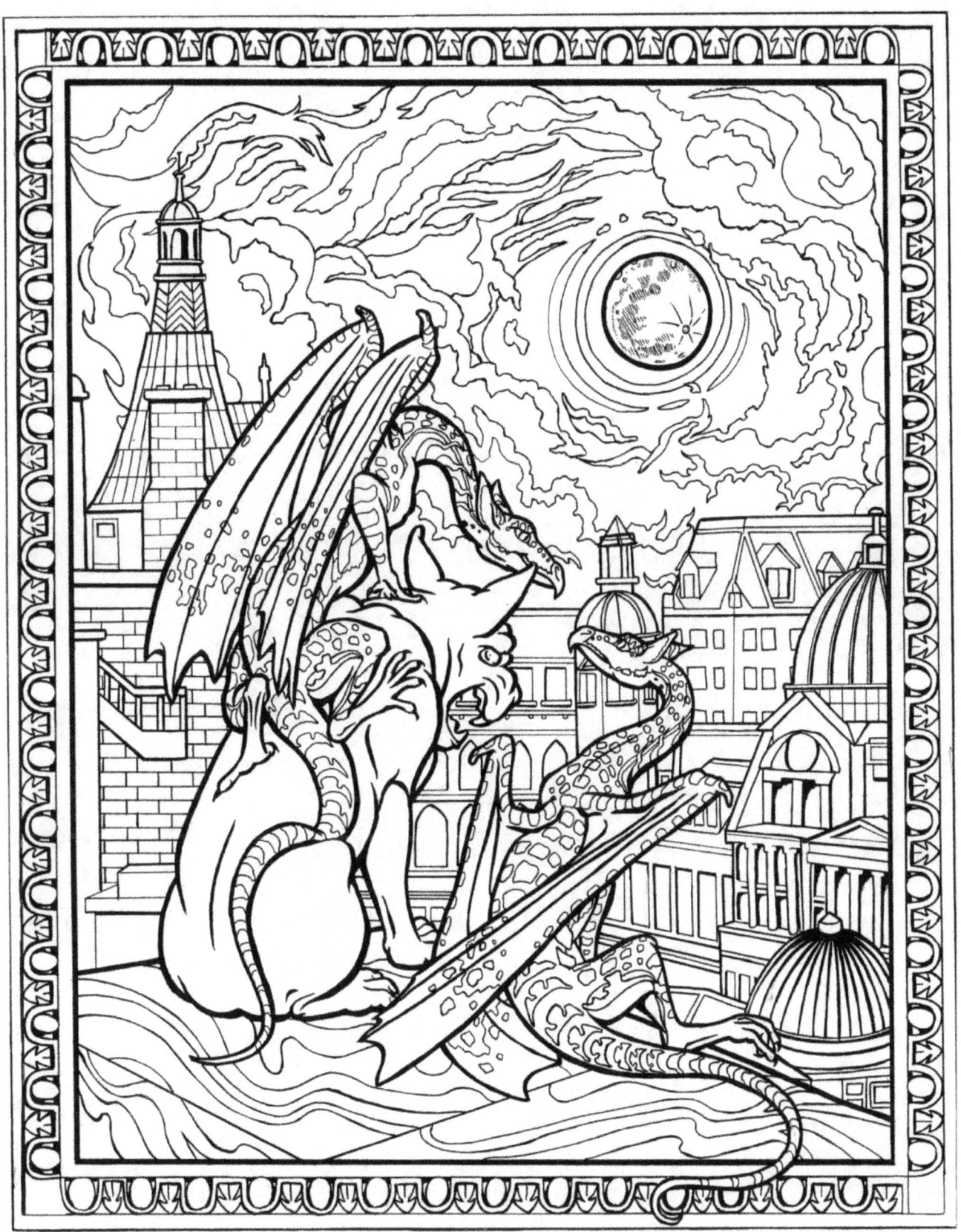

Full Moon Magic
14

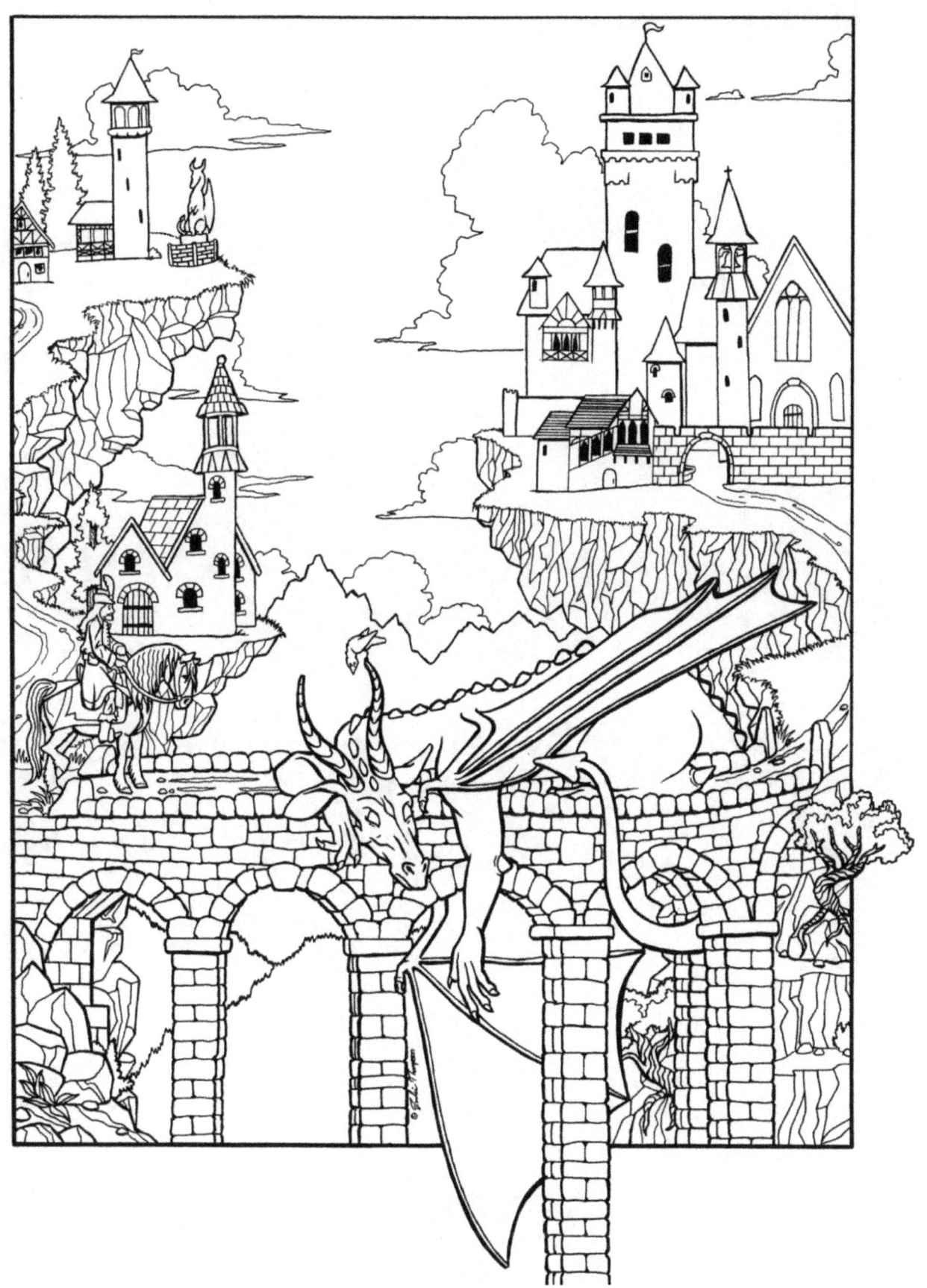

Let Sleeping Dragons Lie

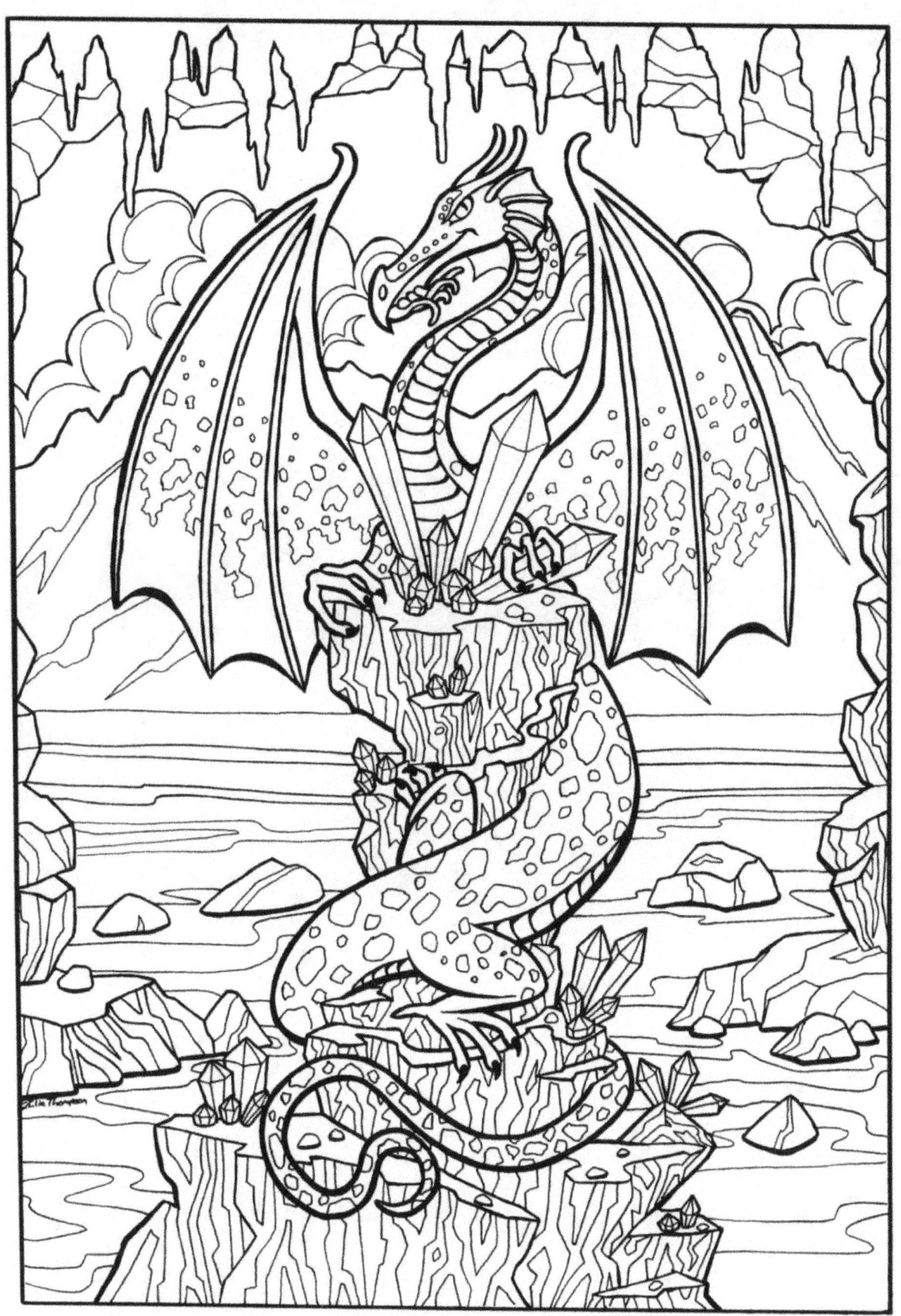

Crystal Cavern
16

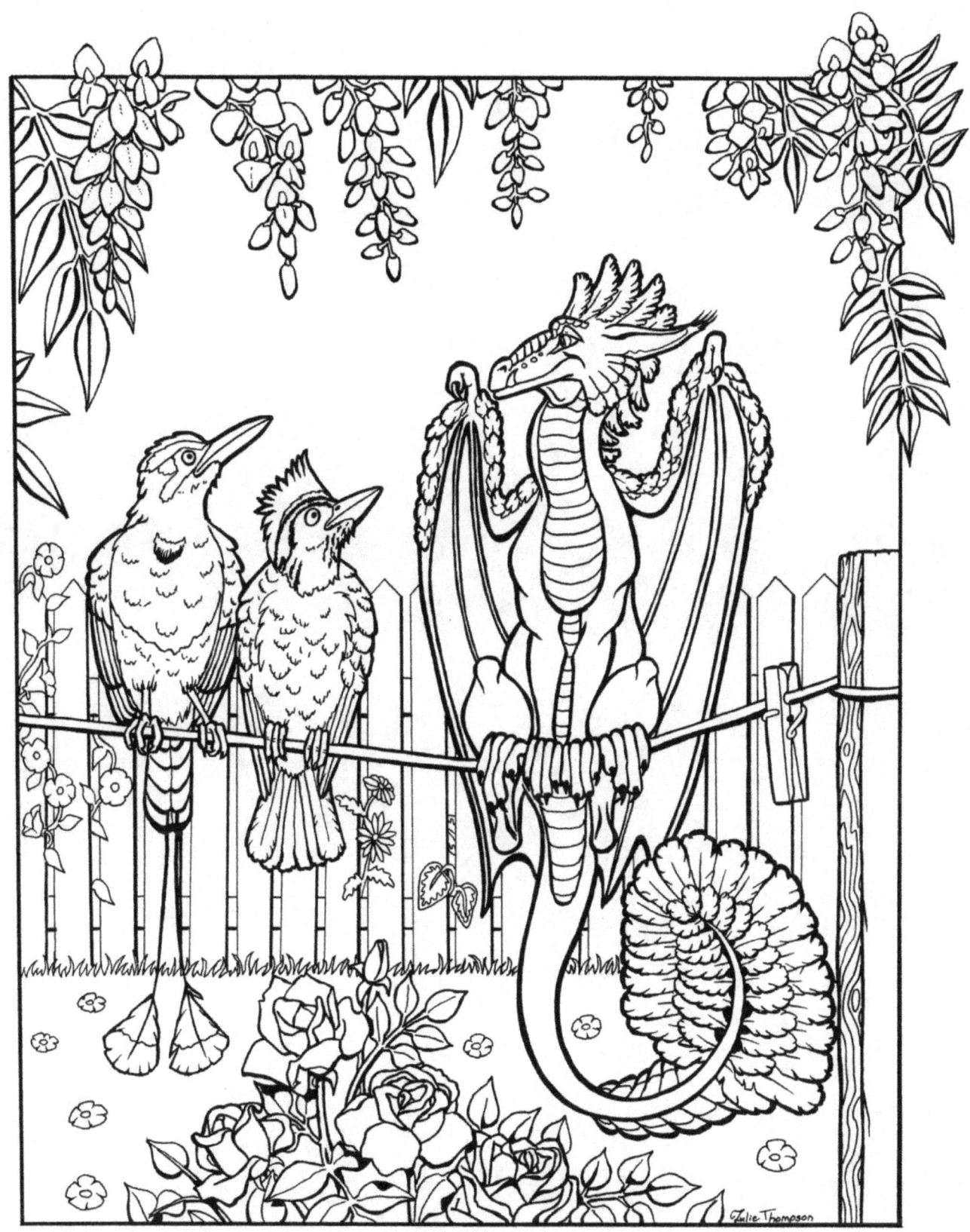

Birds of a Feather
17

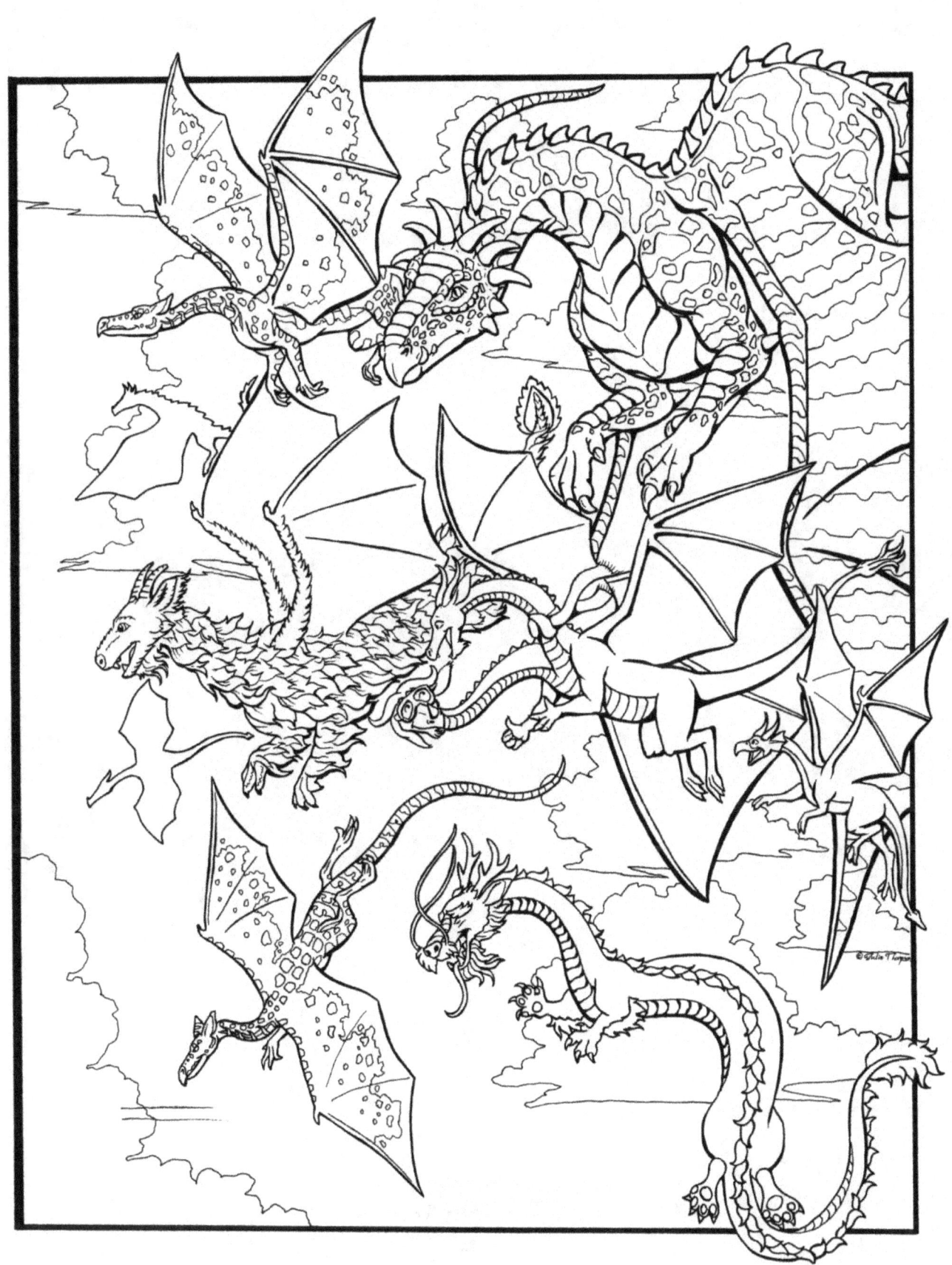

Flight of Dragons
18

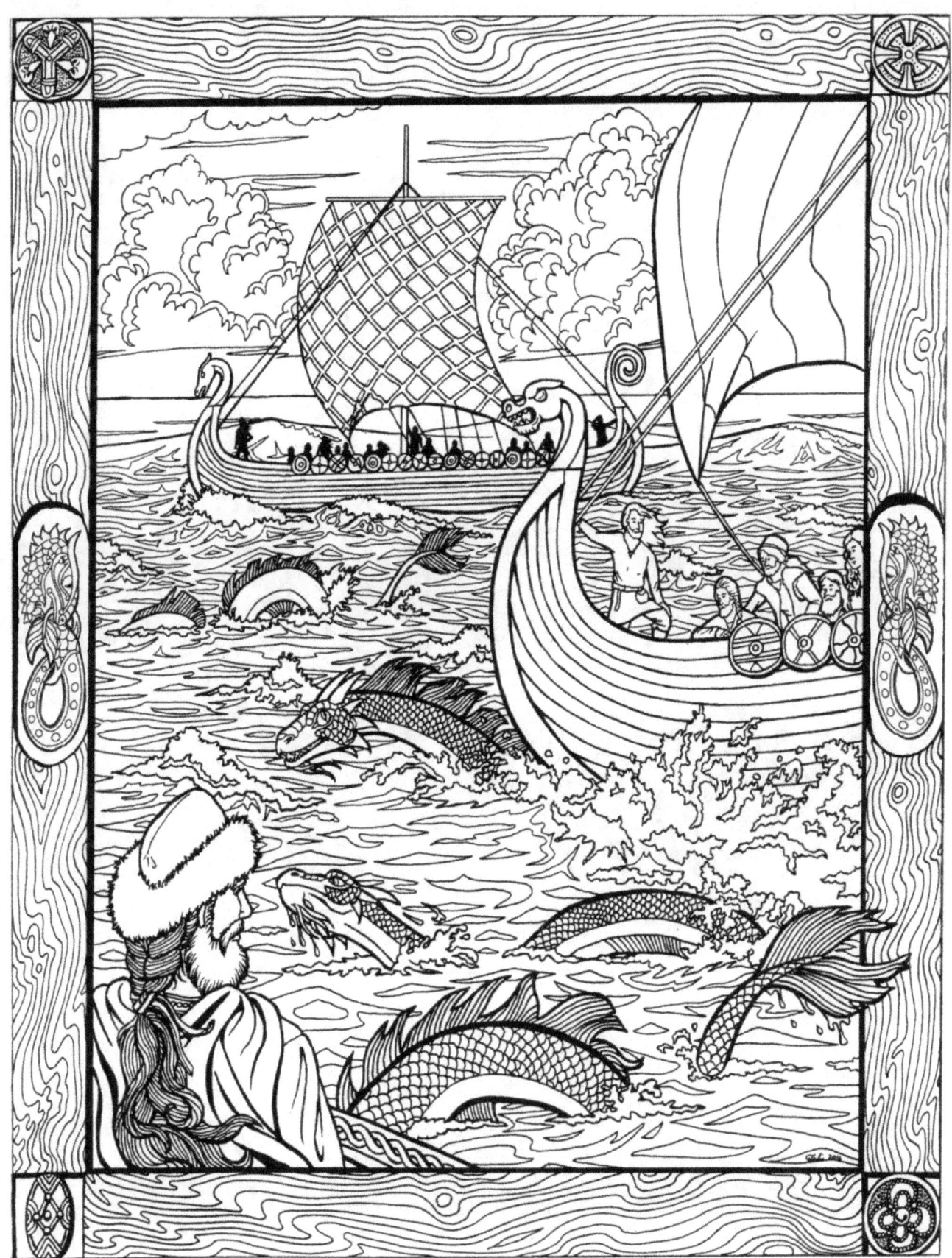

The Wave Chasers

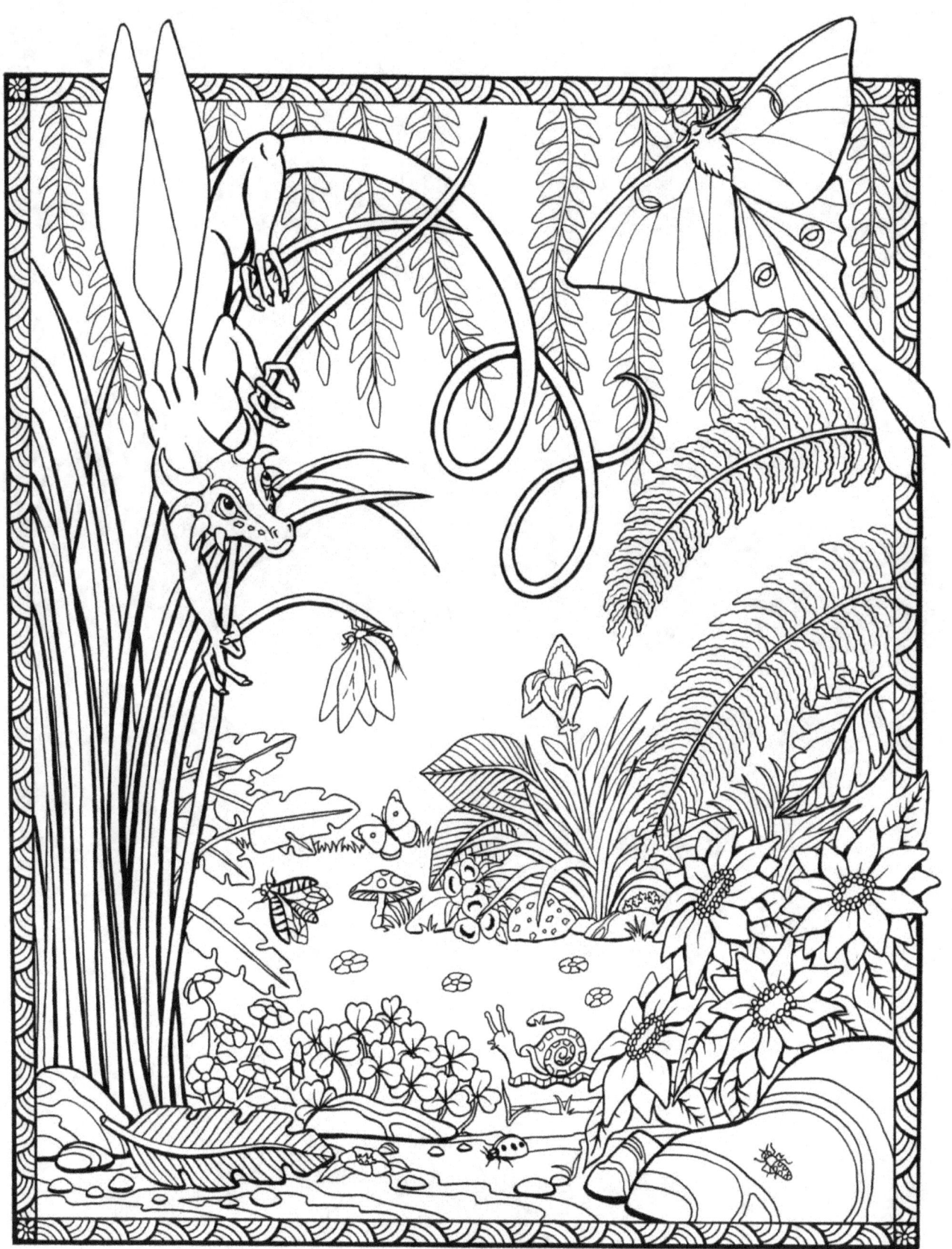

Eye on the Prize
20

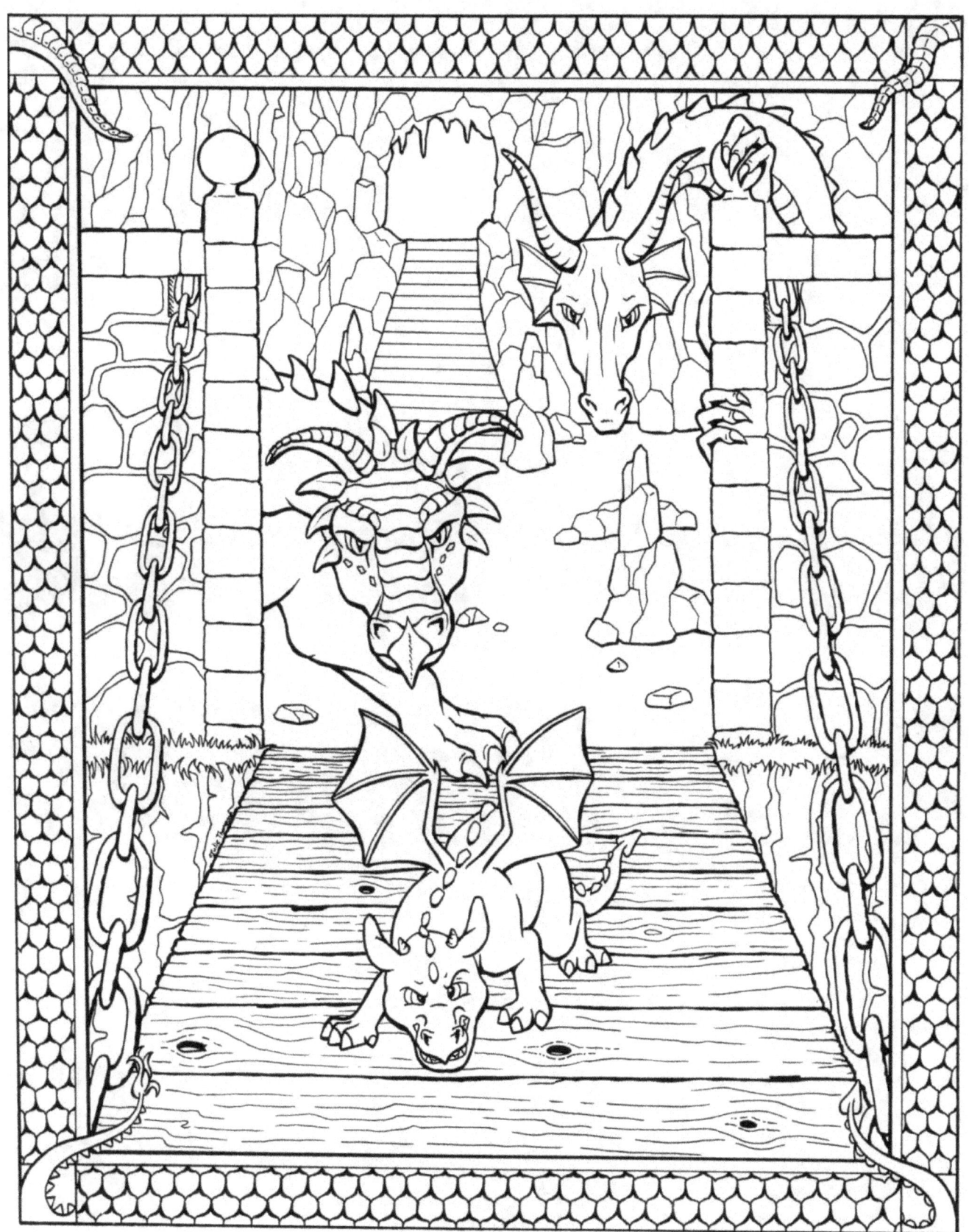

As Brave as Your Backup

21

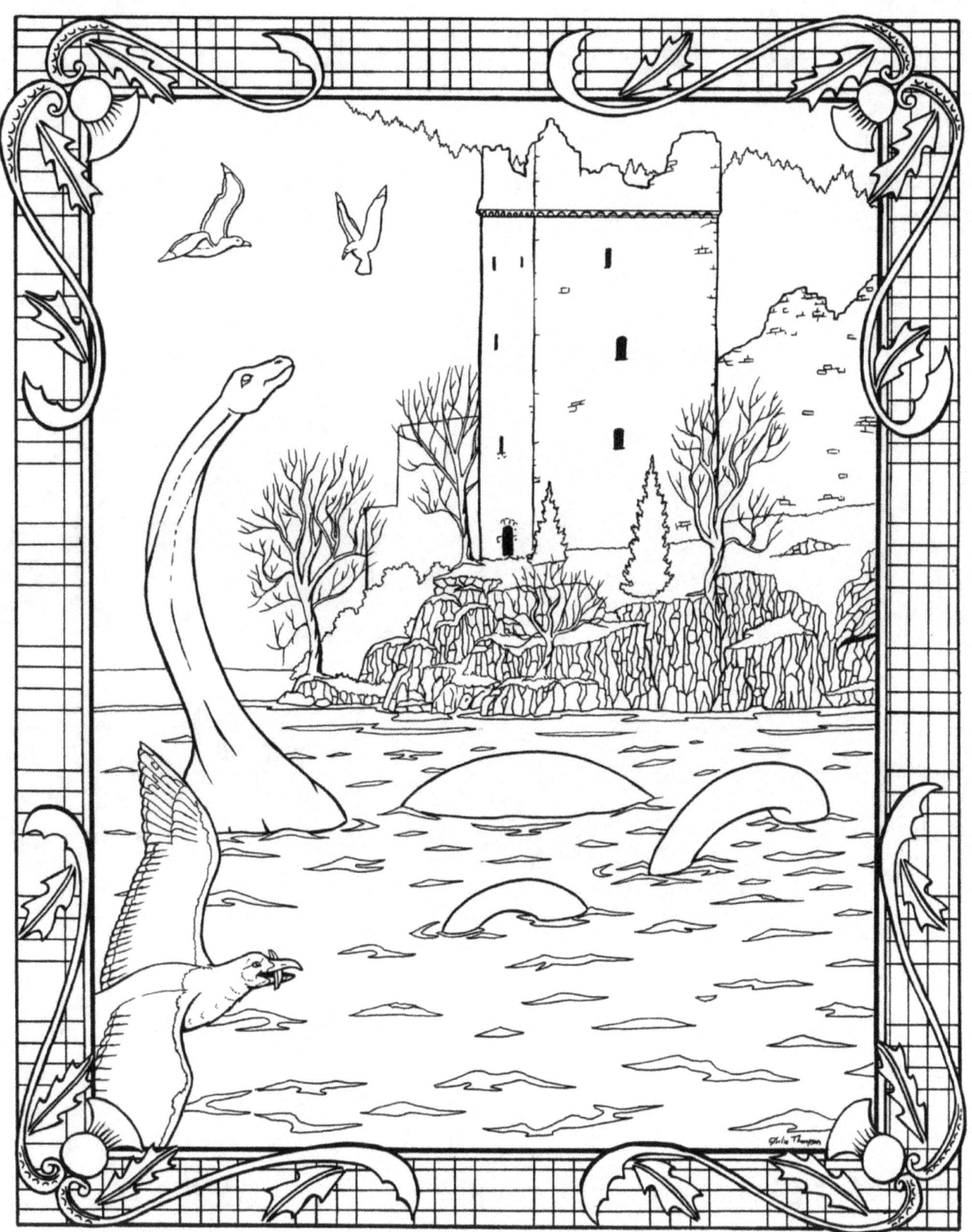

Nessie
22

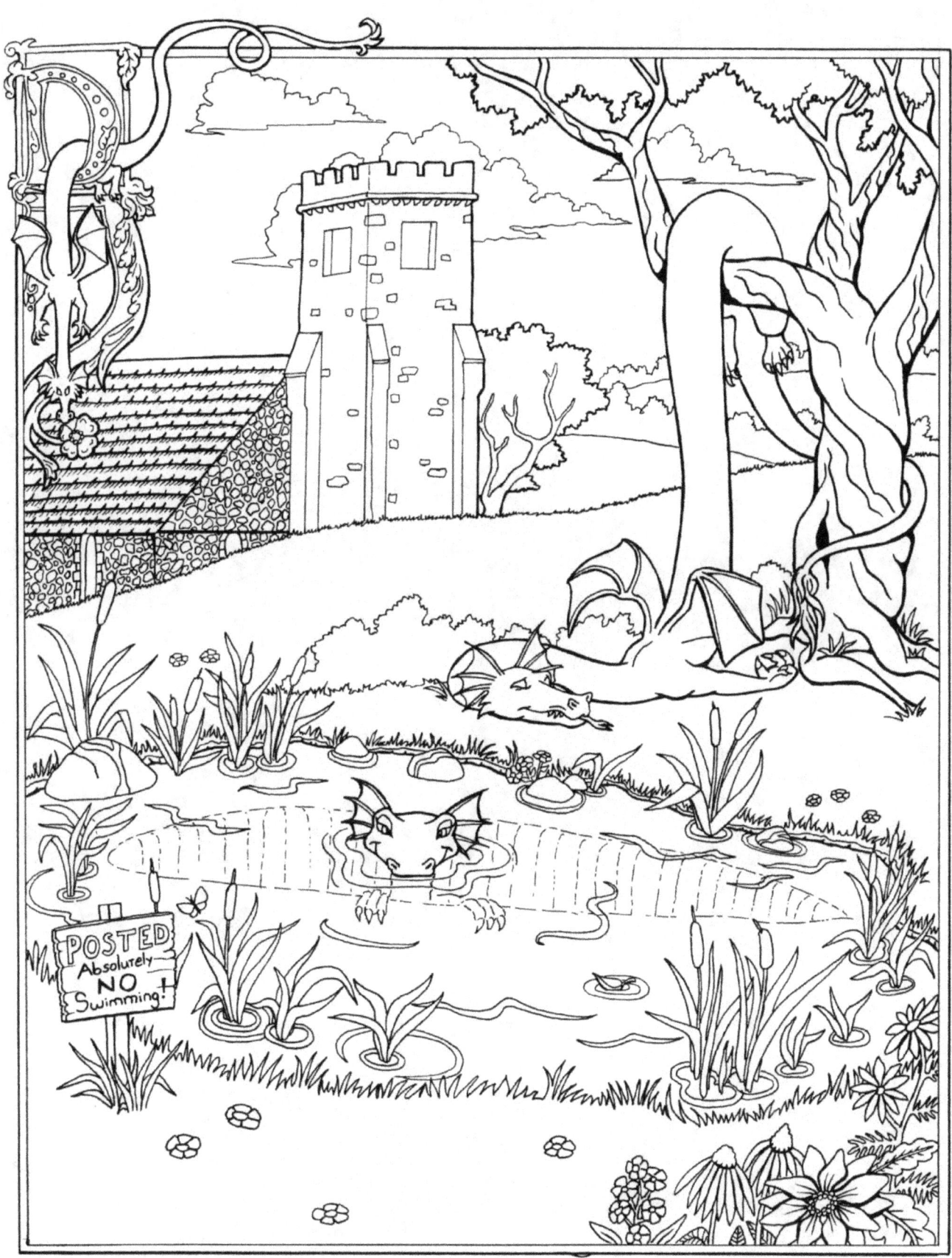

The Knucker Hole

23

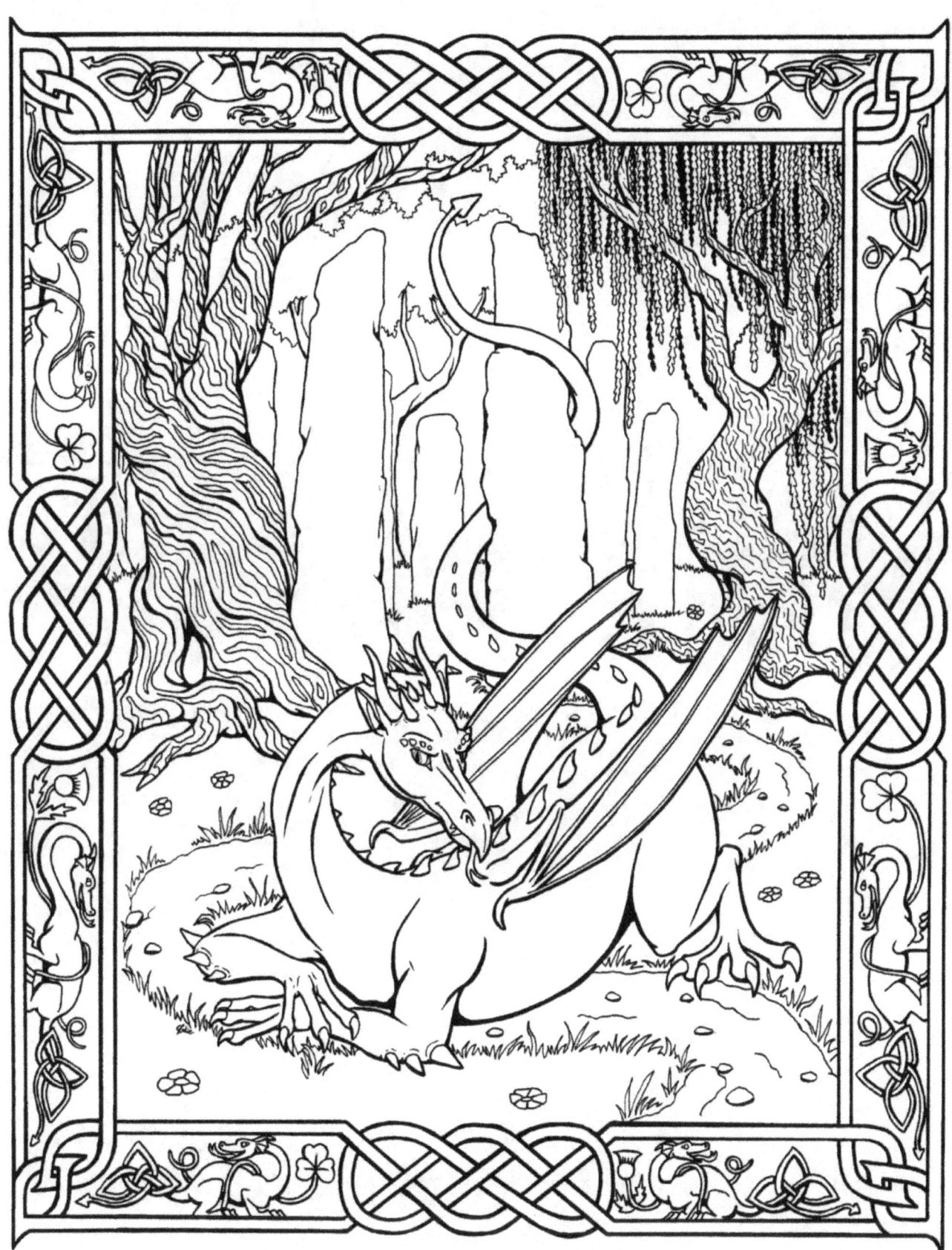

Gatekeeper
24

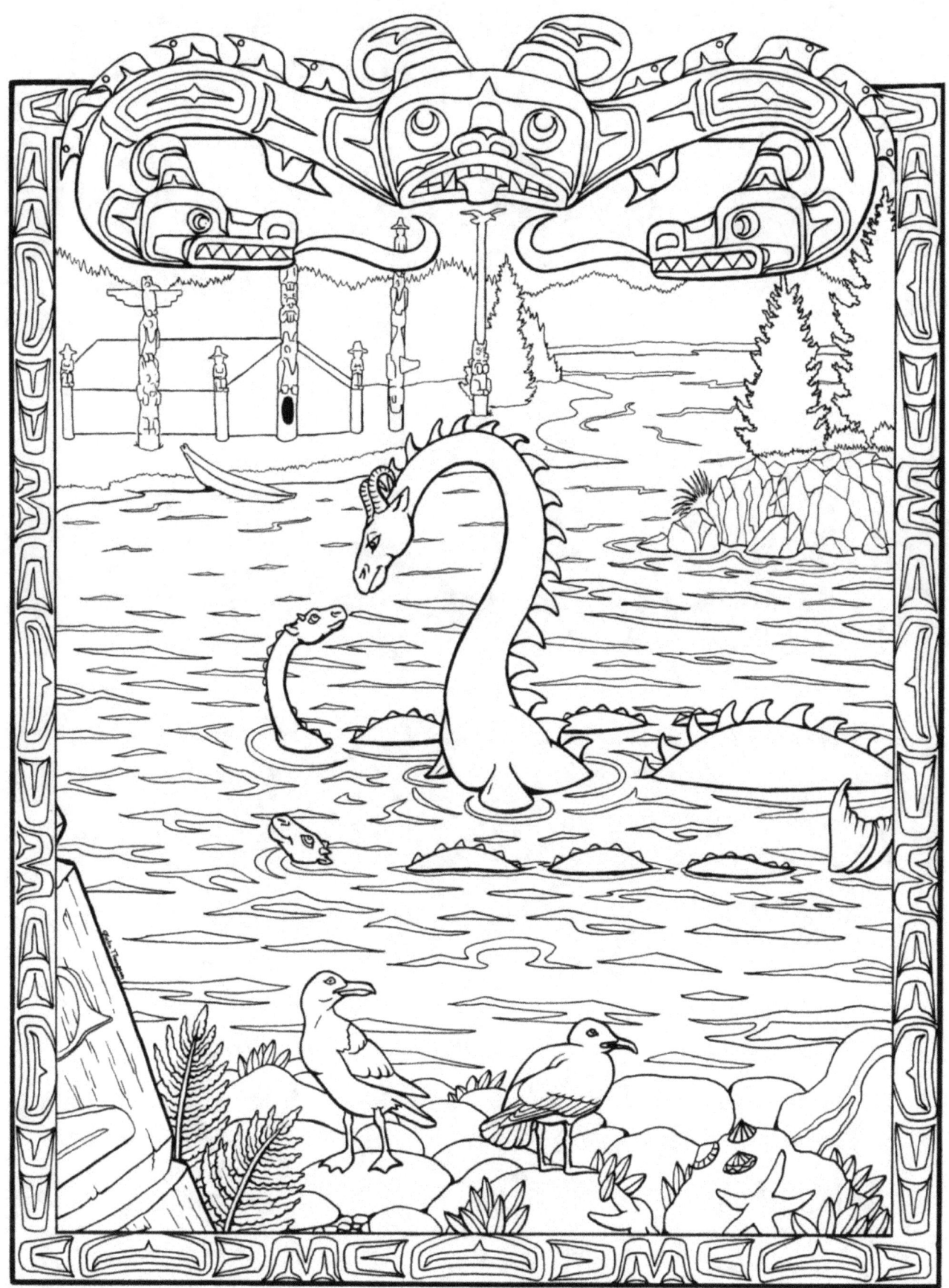

Sisiutl

25

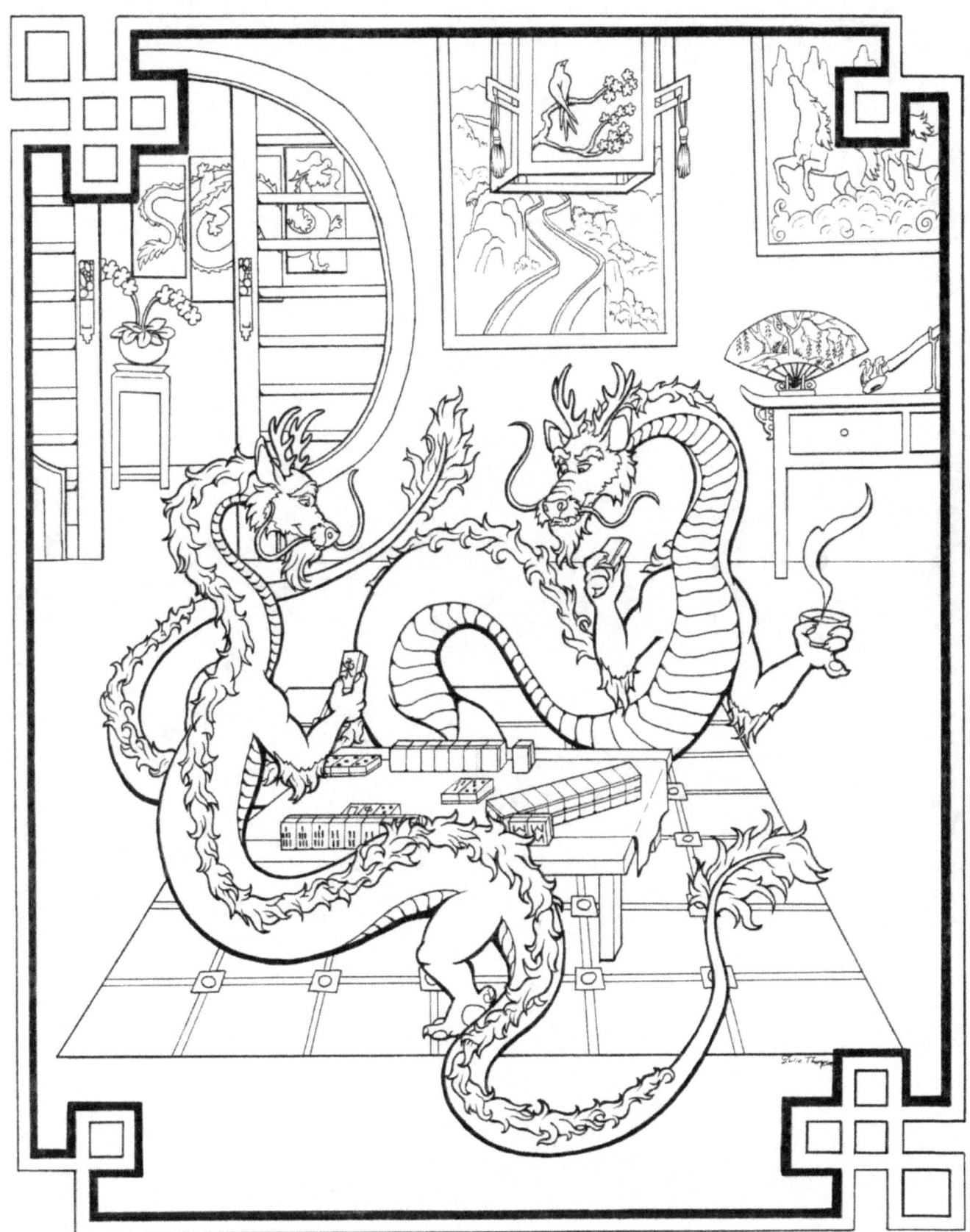

Polite Adversaries

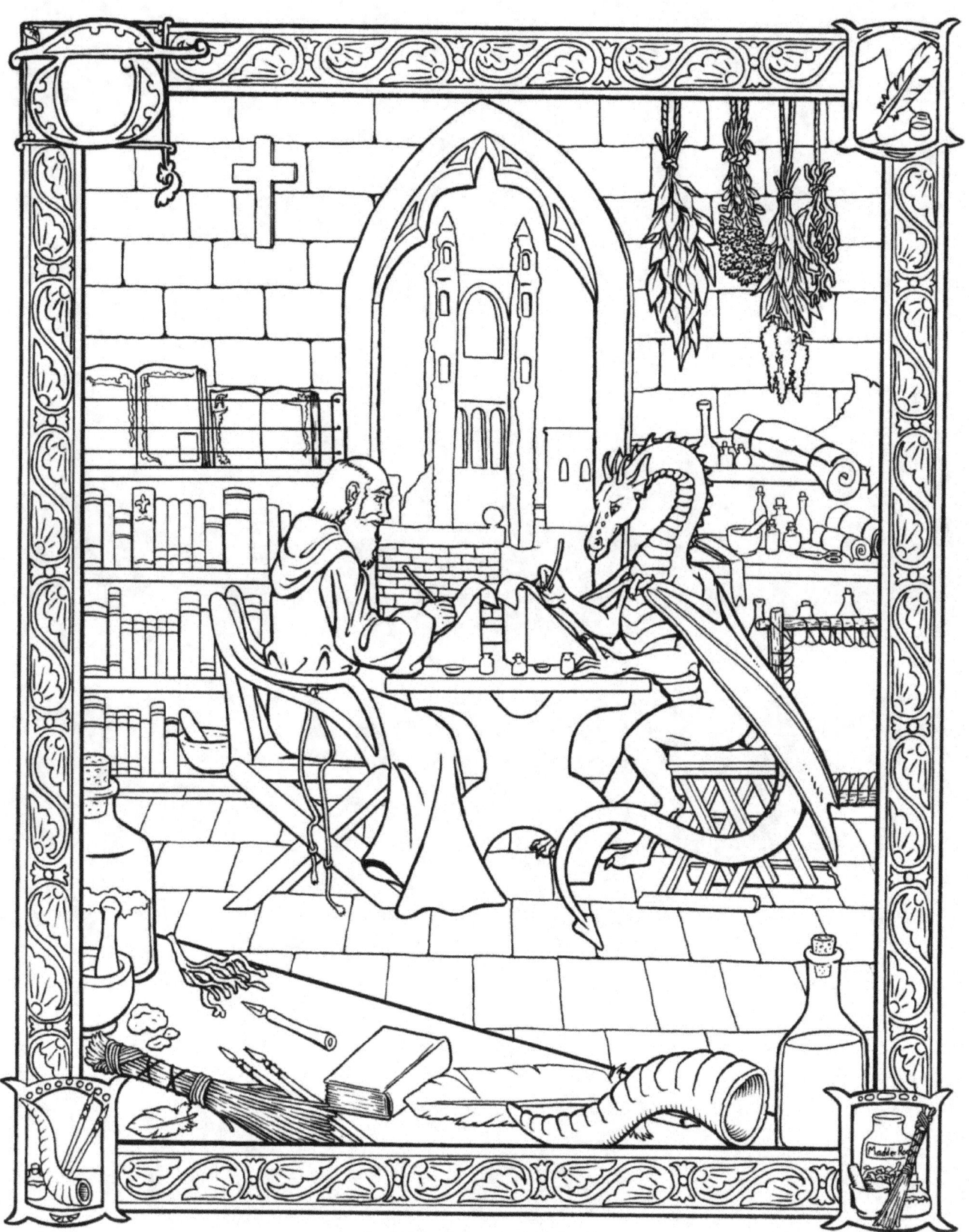

The Illuminator's Apprentice

27

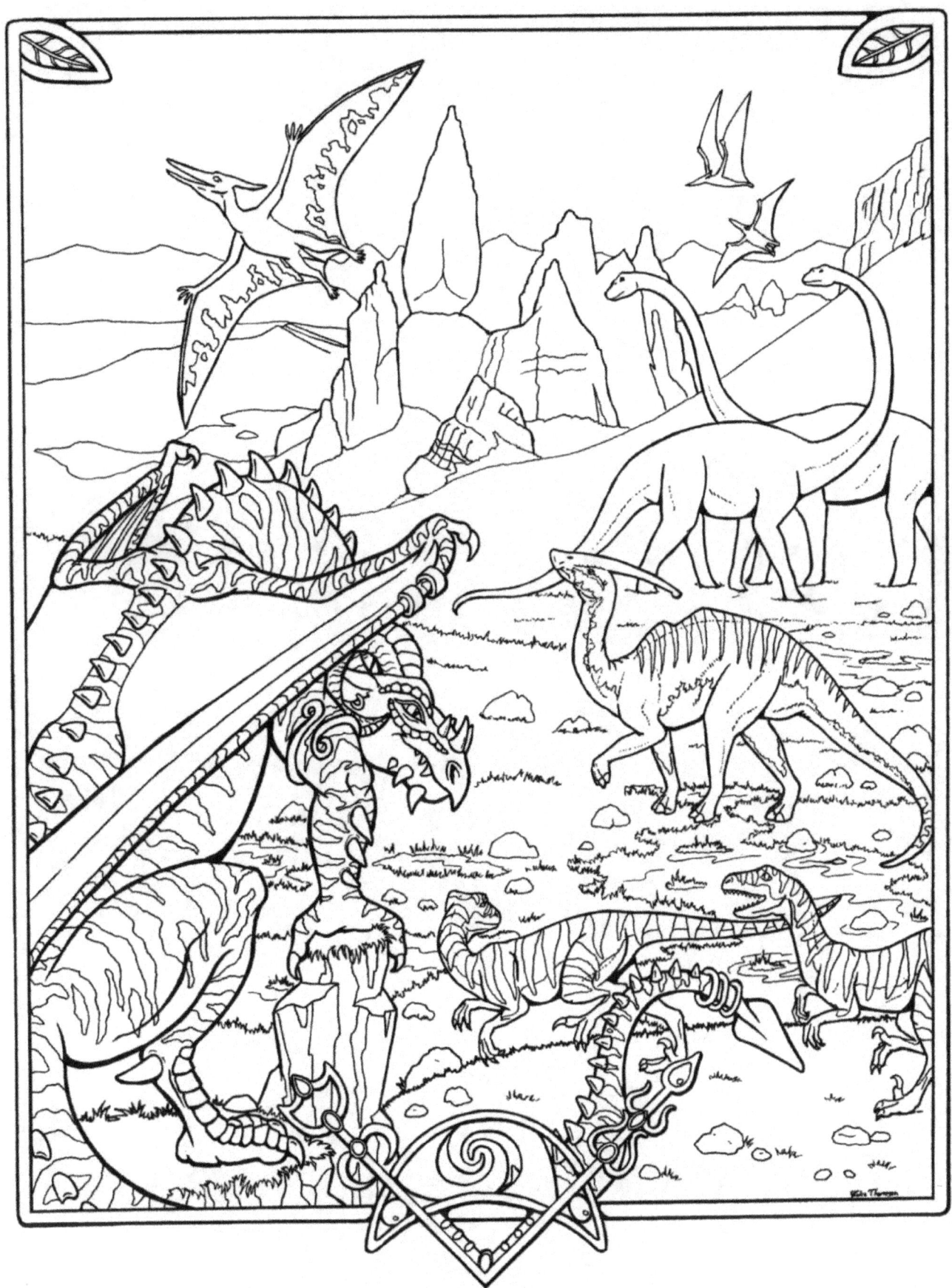

Lord of the Ancients
28

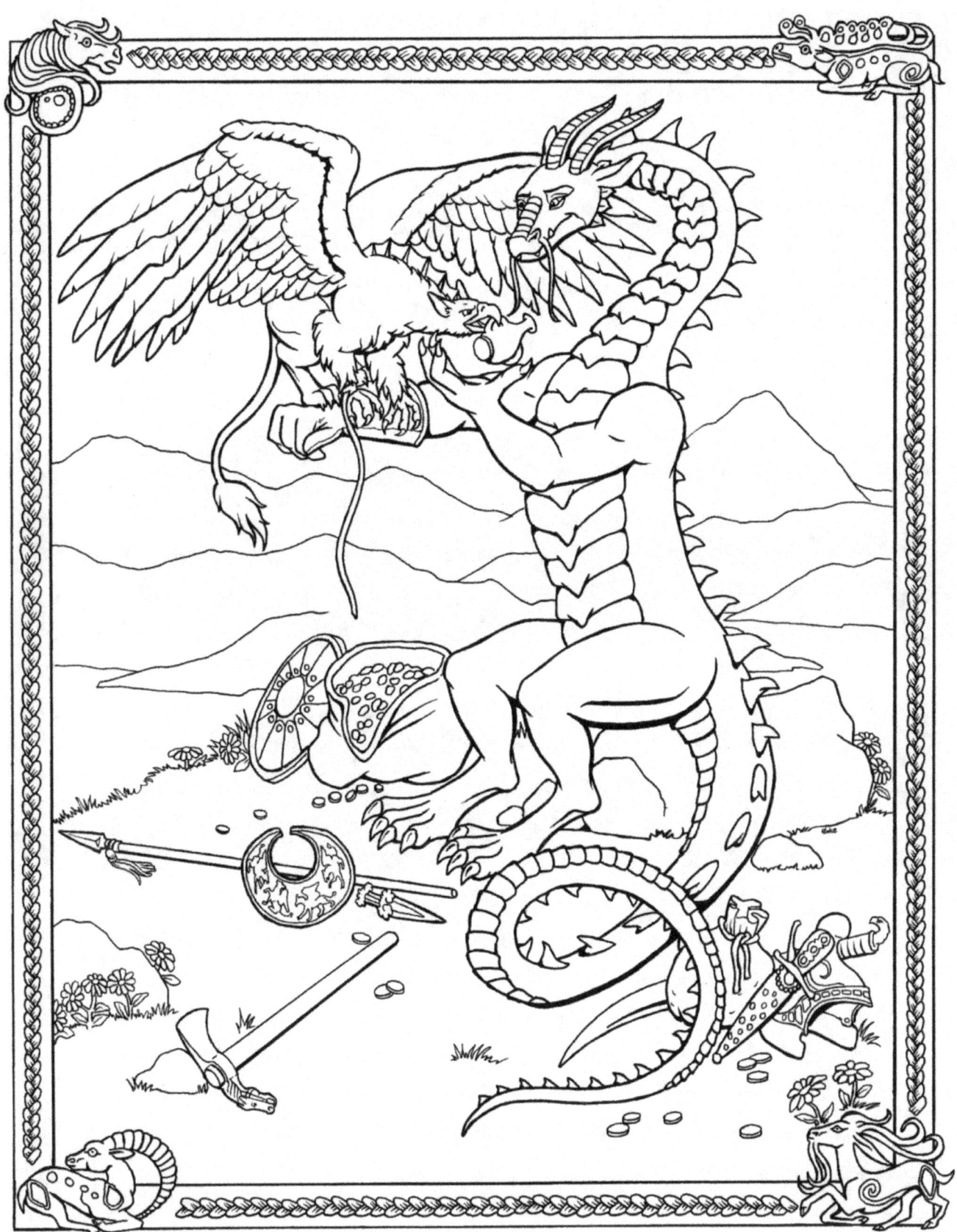

The Huntress
29

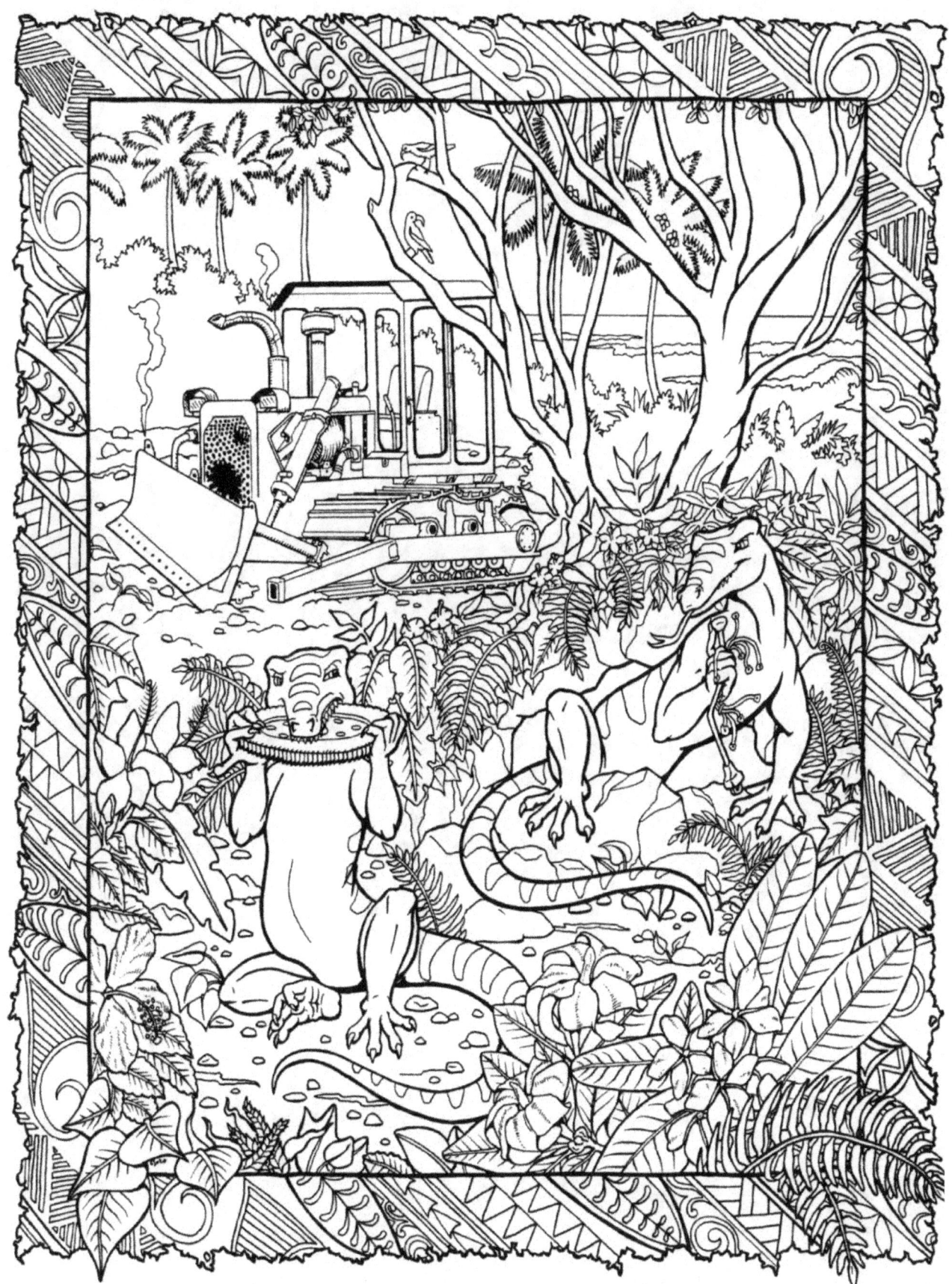

Guardians of Moloka'i
30

The Guardians of Moloka'i

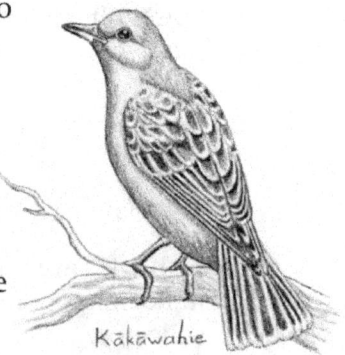

This is the family story told to me by Matt Sproat, Hawaiian musician with the band Waipuna. It is one his Grandmother often told him. Matt's Aunties also shared their memories of the Mo'o of Moloka'i.

Back in the mid-20th Century, back in the 50's or so, there were these two Mo'o who lived on the east side of Moloka'i. These two Mo'o absolutely hated construction and machinery. When these loud machines began to clear the land, the Mo'o would attack the machines and "kill" them.

Matt's Grandmother described how sometimes the Mo'o would wait until dusk, when the workmen had gone for the night. The Mo'o would then come out and attack the unwelcome machines, and successfully "kill" them. The workmen would come out the next morning and find their construction equipment had been disabled.

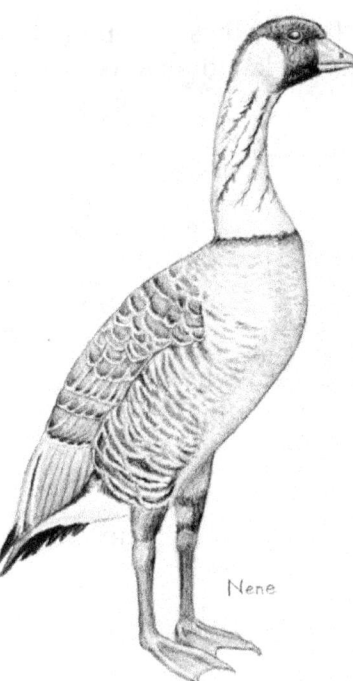

Matt's Aunties also have memories of these fearsome Mo'o, having talked to the workers who operated the bulldozers. As they operated their machines. the Mo'o came up out of the ground and attacked the bulldozers. The workers were so frightened by this fierce attack, they leaped out of their dozers and went home to Honolulu - never to come back.

Mahalo, Matt, for your story!

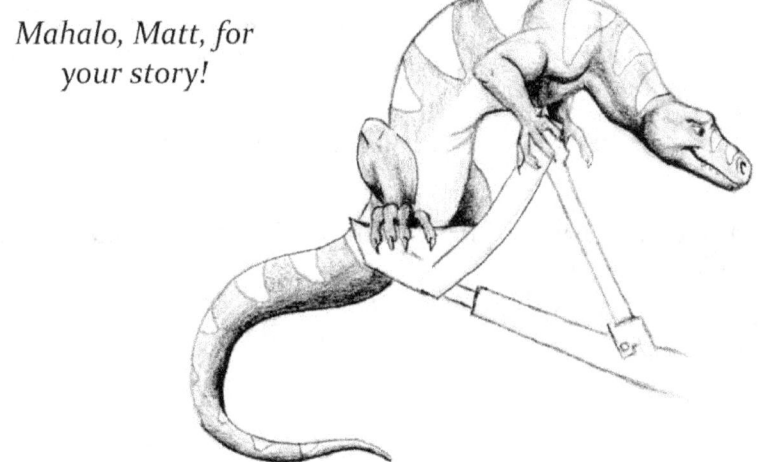

This coloring book is far more than a treasury of fanciful images. There was a tremendous amount of exploration and research involved. An enormous amount of information was gathered as I happily dove down one rabbit hole after another, in pursuit of those little tidbits that would make each illustration truly unique.

To give you an idea of some of that knowledge gathered along the way, here is just a small sample for you to peruse. I hope it provides you with a little more depth into what went into the drawings you now hold. Enjoy!

- There are far more than a couple of types of Chinese Dragons. They could be a book unto themselves.

- The male Resplendent Quetzal looks like an undulating serpent when it flies.

- Epiphytes are numerous, fascinating, and easier to keep than their reputations would have it. Regional floral research for the Quetzalcoatl illustration has turned me into an orchid collector.

- There is a sea monster legend here in the Pacific Northwest from two different cultures in the region. Is it possible that Caddy and Sisiutl are one and the same?

- There are lizards in Southeast Asia whose specialized ribs give them "wings", enabling them to glide over great distances. They can sail over as much as the length of a football field!

- Reptile eyes are amazingly visually complicated and beautiful.

- A group of dragons is called a Flight.

- Red and Blue notebook lines have their origins in Medieval codex production.

- The Isle of Skye in Scotland has a wealth of dinosaur fossils.

- At St. Magdalene's church in Lyminster England there is a stained glass window with a depiction of a Knucker dragon from local legend. As credit to the inspiration for the coloring page you will find a depiction of the church included in the "Knucker Hole" illustration.

- The largest pair of standing stones in a prehistoric Celtic stone circle mark the entry to the circle.

- Most cultures around the world have Dragon legends, enough to produce many more books!

ABOUT THE AUTHOR

Julie Thompson first found worldwide acclaim for her meticulously painted wing feathers. These naturally shed plumes became canvas for all manner of subject matter, from portraiture and wildlife, to historic architecture and landscapes, and so much more. Her work has been written about in over forty countries and collected around the world. Julie has grown up around nature and antiquity, exploring her grandfather's museum and the natural world all up and down the US west coast, from Alaska to California. Her love of research and detail led her to employment in illustrative work and research in archaeology and local history, and then on to her own projects of exploration and documentation. Her latest endeavors have brought her to the illustrative world of coloring books, where you'll find the fruits of many hours of information-gathering combined with vivid imagination, to create some truly unique imagery.

Have you been enjoying this book?
Please consider leaving a review for "Dragon Fancy" on Amazon. The reviews left by you and by others will help this book to be found by other people to enjoy.
Thank you!